MW01656991

MEXICAN WINES:

A guide to fall in love with Wines of México

Literary guide and editorial coach:
Alba Letycia y Deyanira Martínez.
Proofreading: Ivett Villa
Ivettvilla71@gmail.com

Design, layout, and publication by:
Inmersión Digital
Web: inmersion.digital
Email: contacto@inmersion.digital
WhatsApp: +52 55 2887 4632

Martha
Cisneros Paja

MEXICAN WINES:

A guide to fall in love with Wines of México

To my grandparents, *los laguneros*,
and to you from the Balkans

Contents

Prologue

It is an honor and a privilege to be able to write the prologue to this book about Mexican wines. As a passionate winemaker and lover of wine culture, I can say with certainty: this book is a valuable contribution to the world of wine and a tribute to México's wine-growing wealth.

Since I met Martha Cisneros, I have witnessed her deep knowledge and experience in the fascinating world of Mexican wines. Her tireless dedication for discovering and sharing the history, vineyards, grape varieties, and winemaking techniques used in México has been inspiring.

Throughout these pages, the reader will be transported to the beautiful landscapes of México's wine regions, where vineyards stretch out perfectly with nature and also will learn about the grapes rooted in Mexican history and identity, as well as the international influences that have found a new home in these regions.

The meticulous focus on every detail, from the cultivation of the grapes to the fermentation and aging process, will enable the reader to understand the complexity and unique character of Mexican wines.

But beyond the technical aspects, this book is also a tribute to the passionate people dedicated to wine production in México. The viticulturists and winemakers who, with love and patience, work the land and take care of each vine to offer exceptional wines that delight our senses.

As the reader delves into these pages, I'm sure they'll be captivated by the passionate and immersive storytelling. This book will be a reference for all those seeking to dive into the world of Mexican wines and discover the wine jewel that México has to offer.

Congratulations on this extraordinary achievement dear Martha. This book may become a beacon of knowledge and enjoyment for all wine lovers and inspire new generations to explore and value México's wine diversity.

With affection and admiration,
Lulu Martinez Ojeda
Winemaker in Bruma Vinicola

Mexican

wines

vinos

con

alma

Foreword

Mexican wines have a distinctive identity and history apart from the fact that grapevines were introduced to México by Spaniards. This is an important point to remember.

Throughout this book, I want to emphasize the identity of Mexican wines from an international perspective.

Nowadays, Mexican wines celebrate the history of their heritage but also welcome the influence of international perspectives, making it a melting pot of grapes. There are many ambitions and ideas to consolidate the Mexican wine industry. Currently, Mexican winemakers have the opportunity to innovate and create new and unique wine blends. However, they still have to reach an strongest potential within the industry to support their production and trade system, among other challenges.

Although México's millenary culture -Aztec and Maya- was torn apart during the fifteenth century, this great change led to the rising of a new identity: *Los Mexicanos* (Mexicans). Through the search for *La Mexicanidad* (Mexican identity), we overcome battles, treaties, wars, and a massive crisis of identity, so a new perspective was born. The Mexican way is *hacerlo a la Mexicana* (doing it the Mexican style). This Mexican lifestyle is characterized for having an authentic and passionate way of embracing adversity and keep moving on. A common saying in México is: *ándale, dale, siempre adelante,* that is to say 'carry on, go on, always move forward'.

La Mexicanidad is a concept that was first addressed by one of the most notable Mexican writers of all time, Octavio Paz. Paz manifested in the chapter *Máscaras mexicanas* from his famous book "El laberinto de la soledad", the love that Mexicans feel for tradition, or as he calls it, "the passion for the form".

The Mexican identity also extends to what it pertains to in this book: the wines of México. My beloved birth country, México, has produced wine since the 1500s and this is an activity rooted in tradition. However, the Mexican wine industry is relatively new. In the last century, Mexican wines have gone through a renaissance by honoring a "new way" ... *a la Mexicana* (the Mexican way). This Mexican approach has, figuratively speaking, a Mexican soul always looking forward, because in México we say *para atrás ni para agarrar aire* –(backwards not even to gain momentum).

To the eyes of the world, Mexican wines are on the rise; I bet they will become a centerpiece in the Americas in years to come. Through these pages, a review of the history of the wines of México tells the story of their traditions and blend of cultures with the focus on the prominent future. In this book, I also mention suggestions for the wine lover who wants to start a Mexican passion and I encourage you to enjoy it with moderation.

INTRODUCTION

My Mexican Wine Love Affair

It seems very ambitious to state that I know Mexican wines, but is very accurate to disclose that I wrote this book because of the love I feel for them. Like those grapes born in Mexican territory, I was born and raised in México. Thus, through these pages, I aim to share the history of Mexican wines, a bit of its viticulture, and of course, recommend some of them.

This book is my own perspective on the *status quo* of Mexican wines, along with some fundamental knowledge of the regions where these are produced. I hope you enjoy this short tour of the wine regions in this wonderful country through the bicultural and Mexican colored lens and personal experiences.

How did I Come up With Writing a Book About Mexican Wines?

Well, let me tell you a little bit more about me.

I am a wine lover, a wine educator, a wine writer, and an engineer!

You can find me on Instagram at @winedivaa

I was born in Torreón, Coahuila, a city in the North of the country. My hometown is just a couple hours away from Valle de Parras, the birthplace of wine in the Americas, and where Casa Madero winery is located. I visited the winery when I was 15, and I have returned more than once through the years.

During my upbringing in México, wine was not a regular feature at our dinner table. There was beer, *carne asada*, with a heavy Texas influence, as well as boxed wine and barbecue. However, my perception and experiences with wine changed during my college years.

Despite studying for a Bachelor of Science focusing on Computer Engineering, I was a radio host during college. Also, in those years, I was deeply engaged with the underground songwriter movement known in México as *la trova* or *los trovadores.* I organized concerts and promoted songwriters throughout México. Is fair to say I have always supported the underdog. Due to these concerts, I traveled throughout México, from the North to Central region, commonly known as the *Altiplano mexicano*, and during this traveling, I visited some wine regions.

During my time as an international student in Madrid, I was heavily influenced by the Spanish culture. After graduation, I got a job in Barcelona, where wine was often present at business meetings and corporate events. Although I did not initially consider pursuing a career in wine or media, living abroad and immersing myself in different cultures sparked my interest in wines.

Then I found myself pursuing the American dream. I immigrated to America, to New York and Texas. I collaborated with the Mexican Consulate of New York Cultural Affairs Department, offering technology and educational information to the community in the city. Since then, I have become very close to different organizations supporting Mexicans abroad, particularly in New York City.

After some romantic struggles, I met Luan, my husband, and we both connected over wine. I started a blog documenting our findings, which became a second career: media about wines. My interest just kept growing. I completed a Wine and Spirits Education Trust Level 2 certification, enrolled in the Wine Scholar Guild, and most recently, the Court Master of Sommeliers approved me as an Introductory Sommelier. I'm on the waiting list to take the Certified Sommelier exam.

I consider myself bicultural. I live in New York, but my life between Monterrey, México, and the border, gave me perspective and thickened my skin. Because of my love for Mexican wine, this was a sweet place: I got to experience these wines on both sides of the border. On one hand, I was aware of the new waves of Mexican wine, its scene, and festivals in my own country. On the other hand New York City, where I spent more time searching for these wines. As an avid technologist and with the whole world at my fingertips through social media, I was sharing my experience with Mexican wines.

Moreover, through blogging and founding a wine club, I have had the honor to participate in wine events and tasting seminars from different world regions, all hosted in New York City. Therefore, I wondered why I never got an invitation to a Mexican wine tasting. I barely saw Mexican wines on a list at a Mexican restaurant or had a hard time finding them in a liquor store. All those facts made me question the need for more awareness on them, at least in the Northeast of the USA. Texas and California have seen the inclusion of this wines more than New York naturally since they are very close to the south border.

In 2020, during the pandemic, I founded the Latinas Wine Club to initiate an effort in education on this topic focusing on the Latina community. The multicultural vision has encouraged me to become a wine educator.

Photo Credit: Ricardo Hernadez, 2021

I decided to step outside my comfort zone and host events showcasing Mexican wines. Our first event took place in March 2021 during the Covid quarantine. With the help of my team at Latinas Wine Club, we organized a virtual event where 40 wine enthusiasts from all over the country came together to discover and learn more about Mexican wines. I still remember the day I was working with one of my former partners at Latinas Wine Club on the content for our virtual class, and we came together with the title: *Los vinos con alma* (Wines with soul).

Since then, the phrase *"Los vinos con alma"* stuck with me to describe Mexican wines because they have a Mexican soul.

After that first virtual event, we hosted a Latinas Wine Club press and media event as soon as we were able to do in-person events. We called it "French Fiesta", pairing Mexican wines with French cheese at the French Cheese Board, which at the time warmly collaborated with us to host the first event of its kind in New York City's vibrant Soho neighborhood.

Together with the Mexican Consulate, we organized a more official Mexican wine tasting event, focused on educating Mexican restaurants about the industry, in December 2022. This event was top notch as it involved the cooperation of importers, distributors, and the Consul of Economic Affairs in New York. Our efforts helped raise awareness for Mexican wines in New York and received recognition and media coverage.

Photo credit: Pablo Armando Castellanos, 2022

Now, you can already have a copy of my first book on Mexican wines, to which I dedicated a lot of passion and hours. The research for this book was challenging, mainly when it came to wines from Coahuila, where my family is from and the origin of wine in the Americas. I felt vulnerable during the research process finding connections with *Los Laguneros*, the Aztecs from the north, first known as *"Coahuitecans"*. I couldn't help myself remembering my ancestors. On the other hand, I also had a backlash when I contacted some wineries to verify data. Out of respect for their businesses, I will not mention their names. However, it's essential to acknowledge that México needs to make some changes and value free speech. Make known and expand knowledge through communication about these wines from a global point of view is crucial and should be appreciated.

Please, refrain from taking this as a definitive book of what Mexican wine is since it is evolving. Many wine industry folks will agree that currently, México is a melting pot of grapes and winemaking.

However, this book is a first edition resulting from my multiple endeavors to bring awareness to Mexican wines over the past years. The attention on such a soulful region is on the rise. Even, the acclaimed wine critic Jancis Robinson stated that by 2027 Mexican Wine awareness will be in a better place (Williams, J., 2021).

Please excuse me if you see any typos or weird sentences; english is not my first language, and despite receiving outstanding help to provide you with this first edition without ads or sponsorships, it was still challenging. Please let me know if we need to make any corrections, and please share any feedback regarding your experience with Mexican wine or Mexican wine regions by emailing my editorial team at winedivaa.pr@gmail.com

My love for Mexican wines will last forever. Even though there is still so much to do to raise awareness in New York and worldwide, I think I am just contributing two cents.

1.1 How to read this book?

Tell me which wines to taste...

If you want to go straight to the recommendations of Mexican wines, please jump into Chapter 3.

As an aspiring Sommelier, I always have a fixation wishing I had tasted many more labels. Still I suggested that Mexican wine styles to taste are a great place to start learning about those available in the US. However, international distribution is one of the main challenges for the industry in México. Even as a wine professional, getting access to them was a difficult task to achieve.

For the unorthodox reader

If you are interested in the future and the challenges that wines of México face in the global market, go to the last section of this book, Chapter 6, and continue backwards.

I want to fall in love with Mexican wines.

If you want to get the most out of this book, you are at the starting point. Continue reading about the rich Mexican wine's history and immerse yourself in the reading of this book.

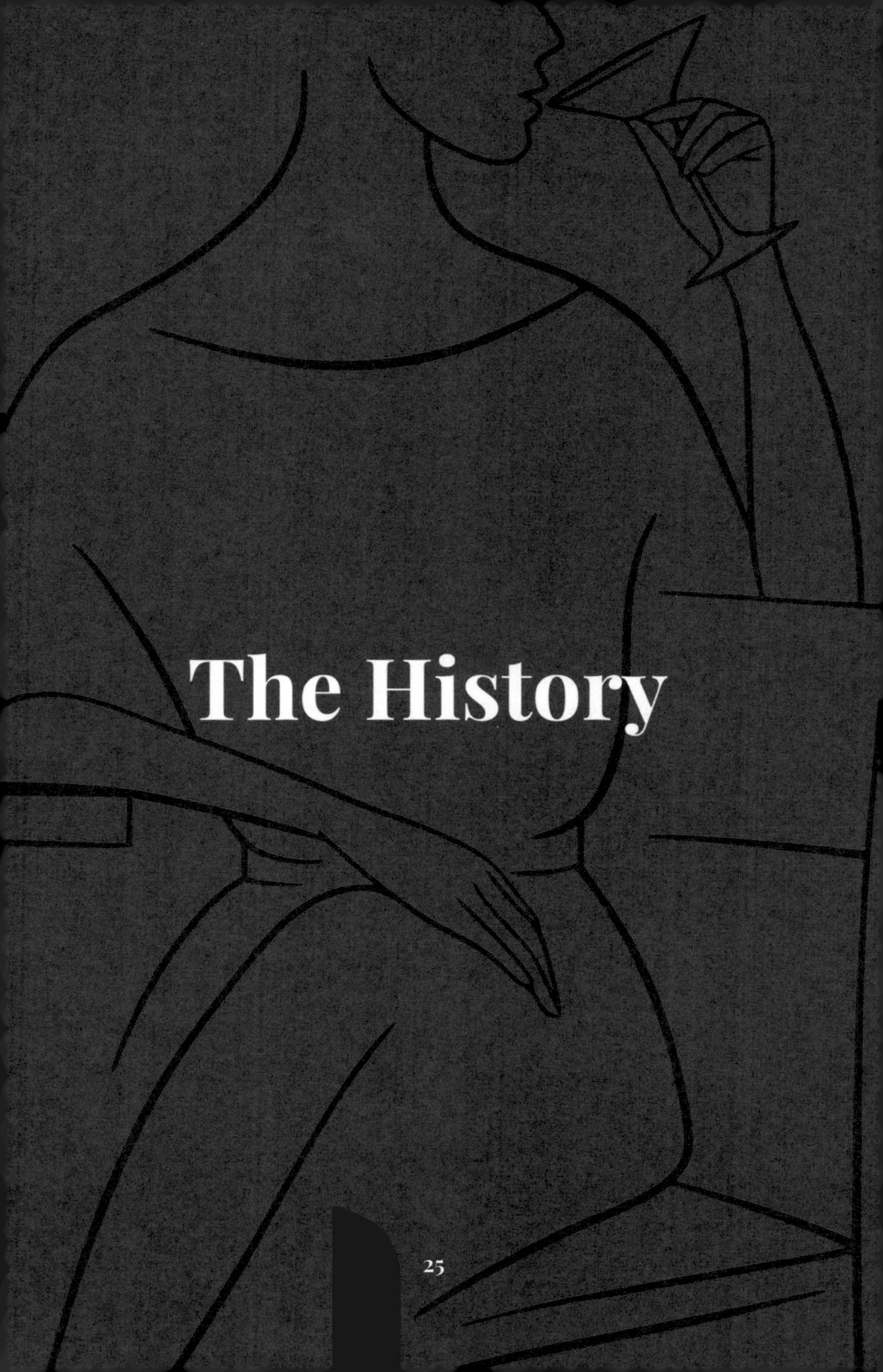

The History

Let's Discover the Origins of Mexican Wine

From the first records of *Vitis Vinifera* towards the end of the Mexican Revolution, Mexican wine went through so many struggles. There are so many fascinating details and I might be missing more than one. Digging into the history has been amazing. I contacted sommeliers and wineries to confirm some details about origins.

2.1 Early Days

"Culture consists of connections, not of separations: to specialize is to isolate". — Carlos Fuentes, Myself with Others: Selected Essays

In México, viticulture started in the Sixteenth Century when *Vitis Vinifera* arrived to México via Spain and settlers ordered local people to start producing wine.

However, there are some bits of history that have been missed. There were another varieties of wild grapes growing in México before the arrival of the Spaniards. According to México City based Sommelier, Alejandra Garduño, who co-hosted the Podcast "Mad About Wine" with me back in 2018, the natives used to prepare a beverage similar to wine using wild grapes. The name of this beverage was *Cache*. Wild grapes were fermented, and fruits and honey were added. I think that's a very significant tale, because the natives were already practicing winemaking, with additives, perhaps. I want to think they wanted to achieve a certain flavor profile. Spaniards brought the proper varietal to produce wine, but creativity and blending was inherently right there with *Cache.*

But let's dig into the facts, because remember that before being a writer, I am an engineer.

2.1.1 *Los vinos de la Nueva España* in the sixteenth Century: From the 1520s to the 1600s

During the arrival of the Spaniards into México, the Jesuit missionaries cultivated the first *Vitis vinifera* vines, the most appropriate grape species to make high-quality wines, between 1521 and 1540. Initially, the grapes were planted in missionary orchards to produce liturgical wines, which is why the seminal variety of viticulture in México is known as the Mission grape.

At the beginning of the sixteenth century, around 1520, the Spanish King Carlos V ordered the planting of a thousand branches of vines and olive trees for every hundred natives.

After the first settlements in Central México, what is known nowadays as México City and surrounding states, the silver rush brought Spaniards to the North: Zacatecas, Coahuila and San Luis Potosí. In particular, and according to John Schmal from *Indigenous México*, Spaniards' initial interest in Coahuila was focused on the region's mineral wealth.

According to "Indigenous Grapes", John Schmal, (2019), "In 1578, Francisco de Urdinola established the town of Parras, which was actually abandoned for a few years, but settlers returned there in 1598. Between 1583 and 1585, an expedition led by Luis Carvajal y De la Cueva, resulted in the foundation of Nuevo Almadén. Other settlements followed in the Seventeenth Century, but unfortunately, no major concentrations of gold or silver veins were found. Coahuila's earth's richness is in metalloids such as iron, carbon, fluorite, and others, which would be discovered much later".

With Coahuila being such a promising estate in the North-East of México, in 1597, Lorenzo García established his Vinícola San Lorenzo becoming The Oldest Winery in the Americas. Therefore, Coahuila became the first region in the Western Hemisphere to plant *Vitis Vinifera.* Nowadays, this estate is known as 'Casa Madero,' and we will be reviewing more details on this iconic winery in Chapter 3.

True or False?

Spanish colonists were believed to be jealous of Mexican wines quality. Therefore, due to México was producing enough wine in 1590, Spanish wine was consumed less than locally produced wine. Out of the rivalry, King Felipe II ordered to uproot all the vines (*arrancadas*).

The history of wines of México is a bit more complex, but at large scale, this is a summary of the origin of *Los Vinos con alma*.

2.2 Modern History

The renaissance of Mexican wines, according to experts, occurred in the last 40 years or so. Mexican viticulture has been modernizing in recent times. Therefore, I call this segment "Modern History", although it must be remembered that Mexican wines have a long and complicated story.

Learning about modern Mexican wine on both sides of the border has been an enjoyable journey, as with everything in wine, there is always more to learn.

2.3 The Beginning of an Industry: 1970-2022

"The preference for Mexican wine in México has changed. The (wine) industry has evolved rapidly in the last fifteen years. Ten years ago, one of the most recognized (wine) brands was, for example, Domecq. Previously, the most popular wines in México were Spanish or from other European countries such as France or Italy. Jeréz was also enjoyed often". — Sommelier, Jorge Barrientos Monterrey, México 2018

I was *suertuda* (lucky girl) to still have connections in Monterrey and great friends who took me to Wine Society México. This is a small boutique wine school that offers tasting classes and wine education. I was introduced to Sommelier Jorge Barrientos, a former Casa Madero representative, who gave me a brief overview during a Mexican Wine Tasting event that roughly summarizes the modern history of Mexican wines and the growing interest of Mexicans in wine consumption. This statement is supported by Mexican Wine Council, which in its annual report for 2022, confirmed that the average annual growth rate of the wine market in México is on the rise; with a growth of 7.07% (between 2014-2018).

One of the critical points that have changed in the modern history of winemaking in México has been the focus on producing quality wines rather than quantity. In this regard, Jorge mentioned: *"Despite México is the country with the longest winemaking history in the Americas (Casa Madero, with 420 years of history), the reality is that the Mexican wine industry has yet to dedicate itself to producing high quality wines. It has only focused on quality recently, in the last forty years or so. For instance, Monte Xanic (winery) and Casa Madero were among the first to venture into or focus on quality".*

In this sense, a step in the right direction was the reincorporation of México in 2016 to the International Organization of Vine and Wine. The OIV (by its acronym in Spanish) is focused on the technical and aspects of viticulture and oenology, operating at the intergovernmental level (OIV, 2022).

Another critical point that Jorge Barrientos shared to understand the modern history of Mexican wines is the increase in domestic consumption. "Approximately since 2010, in México there is a growing trend in the consumption of Mexican wines (...) being of approximately from 30 to 35%, that is, out of every 10 bottles that a person buys, typically three or four are Mexican. The rest are from the rest of the World". (Barrientos, J. 2018).

It is very complex to change the objective to quality rather than quantity, which has given rise to many wineries and boutiques to a movement focused on winemaking without intervention.

Some questions you might still have:

- What changes have occurred in Mexican winemaking to focus on quality over quantity?
- What are some of the opportunities for a growing Mexican wine industry?
- What are some examples of Mexican wines available in the US?

In the following pages, we will delve into more detail about the current situation of Mexican wines.

2.4 Actual Times: The Internationalization of Mexican Wine Industry

According to Secretary of Agriculture, Livestock, Rural Development, Fisheries, and Food (SAGARPA, 2022), in México are cultivated 80 grape varieties approximately; 50% are for industrial use, mainly for wine. During last decade, Mexican wine consumption grew by 20%. Current production only covers 30% of national demand.

Mexican wine is gaining popularity among consumers and for marketing in the US and other parts of the world. Here are three things we should expect soon regarding the globalization of Mexican wines. First, hopefully the United States restaurant industry, and not just those serving Mexican and Latin cuisine, will begin to consider offering wines from México's various wine regions. In this regard, Jeff Harding, beverage director at the Waverly Inn, a well-known mentor to many of us in the New York, recently told Wine Enthusiast that "If you like California wine, you'll like Baja wine" and continued, "These wines are friendly right away". Mexican wines are versatile and can pair well with a wide variety of cuisines.

Second, US retailers will begin to add or expand their selection of Mexican wines, and it will be possible to gain shelf recognition. Labeling Mexican wine sections will become the next significant achievement for the industry abroad.

With the recognition of the US hospitality industry, México will soon be recognized as a wine-producing country. Even so, it will continue to prosper and reach new markets worldwide.

How can I make such a statement? Well, the wine industry in México is expanding. According to the Mexican Wine Council, there are 230 wineries and wine marketing companies in México. These ventures and all those involved in viticulture, hospitality, and travel would immediately benefit from the growing opportunities and awareness around the world. As Mexican wines expand their distribution and export routes, a new market of possibilities opens up. Gabriel Padilla, head of the Mexican

Wine Council, told Mexican magazine Expansion in 2023, that they are committed to produce more Mexican wine and attracting more investments to the industry.

Despite having a long history in winemaking, the Mexican wine industry is fairly new and needs to gain more recognition and overcome the growing interest in Mezcal and its predecessor, Tequila. There are many wine producing regions, which are carving their own *Ruta del vino* (wine route), and are working to create new industries around Mexican wines.

How many wine labels are there in México?

According to sommelier Garduño, there are 50 thousand labels, each one with a beautiful story.

International Influences

Although Mexicans are very proud of their nationality and culture, in recent years, there has been a boom in international influences. In the Mexican wine industry, these influences are no exception. Producers such as Henri Lurton, Parvada, Palafox, and Bodegas Magoni are strongly influenced by European Countries: France, Spain, and Italy, respectively.

Many winemakers have had winemaking experiences prior to their work in México and are applying their vision to the Mexican terroir. Some also advise wineries in addition to play their role as lead winemaking. Such is the case of Daniel Lonnberg, born in Chile and current winemaker at Adobe Guadalupe. He is also the owner of Vinsur wines, located on the road between Ensenada and Tecate, in Baja California. Daniel keeps himself busy, and he is also a consultant for Hacienda Guadalupe, Emeve, and Hilo Negro, among others.

The trailblazer I admire, Lourdes "Lulu" Martinez Ojeda, is a Mexican native who brings a great depth of knowledge into Mexican terroir after spending ten years working in Bordeaux, France. Lulu is a winemaker and partner of Bruma Vinícola and Casa Jippi and winemaking consultant for Palafox. Her first experience after her time in Bordeaux, was to work for the French Mexican wine house Henri-Lurton.

Last but not least, Parvada in Coahuila, among other producers in Valle de Parras, is leading a new movement called "*Nuevo Parras*", embracing Spanish capital and the influence of Lucía García Alonso. We will cover this topic extensively in Chapter 3.

In the eyes of the world, México must be more than tacos, chips and Tequila. The knowledge and opportunities for the Mexican wine industry at an international level are endless. We will discuss more opportunities in Chapter 6: The Future.

White Grapes

Thriving in Mexico

Chardonnay

Baja California
Coahuila
Querétaro

Chenin Blanc

Baja California
Querétaro

Sauvignon Blanc

Baja California
Querétaro

Moscatel

Coahuila
Zacatecas

Italia

Zacatecas

Saint Emilion

Zacatecas

Red Grapes

Thriving in Mexico

Cabernet Sauvignon

Baja California
Coahuila
Querétaro

Merlot

Baja California
Coahuila

Syrah

Coahuila

Tempranillo

Baja California
Querétaro

Carignan

Ruby Cabernet

Salvador

Zacatecas

Mexican Wine Regions

Vineyards are growing in different parts of the country under the Mexican blue *cielito lindo*. According to the Mexican Wine Council, as of 2022, México has 32 thousand hectares, and 15 states produce wine, each one with sub-regions.

How many wine regions are there in México?

Baja California produces 75% of all wine, then Querétaro, Aguascalientes, and Coahuila are the most popular.

These regions have also been working diligently for more than 30 years to develop solid export strategies and participate in international competitions, so Sommeliers and Tasters from around the world have noticed how Mexican wines are thriving in the wine industry. However, we have a long way to go on the consumer side.

In order to present México's wine regions and to reveal those that are rapidly flourishing, I have devised a way to divide them into Baja California, North and Central México. I have also created a section to further discuss emerging wine regions, not based on how long they have been producing, but on the information available based on my limited research.

The North

"The glass frontier" — La Frontera de Cristal, Carlos Fuentes

The love I have felt for this region since I was born has strongly influenced me to describe this region, so be aware!

Please note that I did not include Chihuahua as part of the North wine regions of México, despite it is actually located in this area, but I considered it in "Many More Mexican Wine Regions" of this chapter.

Without further preamble, get ready to fall in love with the Northernmost part of the Mexican wine regions.

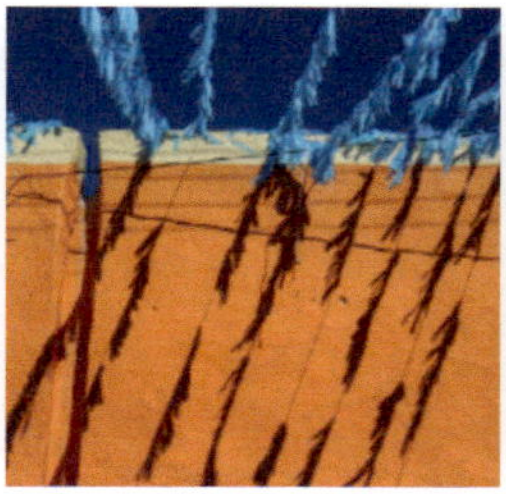

Coahuila

27.0587 °
N, 101.7068 °
W

3.1 Coahuila

Being a *norteña* (a person from the north), I am very familiar with *las carreteras del noreste de México* (Mexican north-west highways). So, grab a bottle of *Vinos de Coahuila* and let's raise a toast to the State home of the oldest Winery in Latin America: Casa Madero. And let's also make a second toast to Coahuila, my birthplace, which has become one of the most important wine regions in México!

My First Visit to Casa Madero

I was fifteen years old when I first visited Casa Madero Winery or any winery at all. It was a fun, unexpected adventure, and an eye-opening experience.

We lived in Monterrey because my dad worked there as an engineer. Part of my extended family lived and continue to live in *La Comarca Lagunera* -the region labeled by Spanish that encompasses three sister cities: Gomez Palacio (Durango), Lerdo (Durango) and Torreón (Coahuila). Thus, we were on the road twice a month for family gatherings.

Casa Madero, the first winery in the Americas, is located in Valle de Parras, Coahuila, about an hour east of Torreón. Torreón is my home town. I was just born there, but I never lived there. That is why it has been so difficult for me to describe where I come from.

I always felt more like *del Norte*, than from the city. I had never lived in Coahuila, but despite living in Monterrey, I never felt myself as a *Regiomontana*. I wasn't from here or there, and I think that is an important part of my identity, being from a region rather than a city.

But let's get back to Casa Madero's first visit. Neither my siblings nor I were dressed nor prepared for the occasion; we were in pajamas. As I recall, my dad took a wrong turn on our trip from Torreón to Monterey, and suddenly, we were in Valle de Parras. '*¡Estamos en Parras, vamos al viñedo!*' (we are in Parras, let's go to the vineyard!). It felt like an extraordinary moment in my life, and I couldn't understand it until later. The best things happen to you when you are in pajamas.

This is the picture my dad took while our first visit to Casa Madero in Valle de Parras. Photo Credit: Moises A. Cisneros Mosqueda, 2007

Since I was a minor, I was not able to taste any wine at all. However, we enjoyed the historic winery tour, and it felt like something rustic and exquisite that we were not used to, but it was magical to be there. It must have been December, during the Holidays, so the high elevation of the area with strong winds felt like chilling, for sure. I still remember *el olor a tierra mojada* (wet earth smell), it must have rained a day or two before.

Here, strong winds and high altitude wines grow.

Fortunately, I returned to Casa Madero in 2017, when my sister got married at their beautiful and historical estate and this time I tasted the entire portfolio!

Important fact

The oldest winery in the western hemisphere, Casa Madero, is located in Valle de Parras, Coahuila.

Location

Coahuila de Zaragoza, -official name of the State of Coahuila- is located in the Northeast of México, bordering with Texas. According to the Texas Del Rio–City Department of Transportation, the Acuña International Bridge, opened in 1930, connects Del Rio, Texas with its sister city, Ciudad Acuña, in the Mexican state of Coahuila.

Its terrain is characterized by its roughness, which includes mountains, hills, valleys, and canyons that stretch throughout the region.

Elevation

Most vineyards are located between 2,300 and 8,700 feet above sea level.

Terruño

The predominant soil types include clay, limestone and sand.

Wine regions

According to the Coahuila Tourism Agency, Coahuila's best-known wine region is Valle de Parras, but there are nine other wine regions in the area: Saltillo, Ramos Arizpe, Arteaga, General Cepeda, Cuatro Ciénegas, Torreón, Múzquiz and Piedras Negras.

Grapes

- Red grapes: Cabernet, Cabernet Franc, Caladoc, Malbec, Pinot Noir, Cabernet Sauvignon, Syrah, Tempranillo
- White grapes: Chardonnay, Chenin Blanc, Muscat de Alexandria, Verdejo

Wineries

There are approximately 35 producers in the region. Currently, according to Selección México, there is a designation of origin for the wines produced here.

"Vinos de Coahuila" brand was created as an organization that currently integrates 28 wine houses from the five regions; strategy that has allowed the entity to position itself as a national and international benchmark in the production of high-end wines, which today competes with the best in the world, turning Coahuila into a wine region of excellence.

"Being the Birthplace of Wine in the Americas is worth saying that its producers have clearly thought about their future preserving the legacy" — Selección México by Concours Mondial de Bruxelles, 2022

Below you will find information about some of the most outstanding wineries in Coahuila.

Casa Madero

Located in Valle de Parras, Coahuila, in the Northeast of México, is the oldest winery in the Americas. Today, it remains the property of the descendants of Francisco I. Madero, a notable former president of México, son of Don Evaristo Madero and patriarch of *la familia Madero*, who purchased *Hacienda San Lorenzo* in 1893.

Casa Madero is currently exporting their Ensemble wine blends to California, Texas and other parts of the South of US. I look forward to hearing that it is available in the Northeast of the USA and other parts of the world.

International press and Sommeliers have recognized many of their wines worldwide. I love their Ensemble 3V, 2V, and V series of wines. The numerical character shows the number of grapes included to make the blend. Letter V represents the grapevine. Its Cabernet Sauvignon Reserva, 3V Rosé, and Chardonnay are highly recognized wines in México or its entire portfolio. Wherever you find a Casa Madero wine, please do yourself a favor and get it; 425 years of experience in the making!

I know they are available in Texas, and I am so jealous! I cannot wait to see them available in the best restaurants in New York and other capitals of the wine world to which they belong.

CASA MADERO
V

Nuevo Parras

In the last three decades, *el Pueblo Mágico* (Magical Town) of Parras de la Fuente, Coahuila, has grown significantly in the influx of tourists who demand more attention to their needs. The gastronomy, the cultural theme, and the Wine Route continue to drive the growth of Parras in the coming years.

Bodegas del Viento

Its name in English evokes 'Cellars of the Wind' literally because it gets windy around its mountain range. They are pioneers in the wine region around the mountain known as Sierra de Arteaga. According to their website, they make high-altitude wines due to the wine region in which they are located, and their wines are intended to evoke quality, exclusivity, elegance, and dynamism. They are known for their Merlot, Pinot Noir and Red blends. Unfortunately, I have not seen their wines in the United States.

Bodegas Los Cedros

A vineyard with a century of work in the land of Coahuila. In 1911, Rosendo Dávila bought the estate where *Rancho El Cedrito* is located in Sierra de Arteaga, where five generations have lived. In 2009, Rosendo A. Villarreal encouraged his children to plant a vineyard and produce high altitude wines, and thus Bodega Los Cedros was then founded. Currently, they focus on a few grapes such as Malbec, Pinot Noir, and Chenin Blanc. I have yet to see their wines available in the US.

Rivero Gonzalez also known as RGMX

The internationalist vision is what has characterized the Rivero Gonzalez Family. María Rivero González is the leader of the family organization of RGMX and RGNY, a winery located in the Long Island Wine Country, New York. María has led Rivero González to position itself in México as a family of wines focused on quality during the elaboration of 100% Mexican artisan products made in Parras, Coahuila. I have had the opportunity to meet Maria and visit both vineyards in Valle de Parras and Long Island Wine Country. Her attention to detail and strategy have impressed me the most about her productions.

In the United States, you can find such wines produced in Coahuila as RGMX Blanco, which is a Cabernet Sauvignon Noir, RGMX Red Syrah, Cabernet Sauvignon, Merlot, and an completely unique orange wine, which I will talk about later in the chapter on the ten styles of wines that you have to taste to get to know Mexican wine. In the near future, importers' portfolios will include more of their Scielo series.

RGMX has also been characterized by offering a personalized service, generating wine experiences around events in its wineries, and pairing its wines with its artisanal and local products from Coahuila, such as nuts and dried fruits that abound in Parras.

Vinos Parvada

This wine project located in Valle de Parras expands to be comprehensive. Vinos Parvada is investing in the vision and potential that Parras envisions for the future. The design firm

Latitud 25 created a comprehensive project that includes a country-type subdivision called *Pueblo,* a concept of 2, 3, and 4-bedroom villas, a boutique hotel, and a representative winery of its label. This resort is meant to be a joyous escape for couples, friends, or the whole family to enjoy the holidays or a wine weekend experience.

In addition to this great comprehensive project, the winemaker in charge of Vinos Parvada, Lucía García Alonso, has impressive experience for her young age. She worked at Lapostolle and Montes Alpha, two of the most important wineries in Chile. She has a degree in Biology and a Master in Oenology and Viticulture from the Polytechnic University of Madrid, training and working in Jerez, one of the oldest and most recognized denominations of origin in Spain.

I had the opportunity to taste Parvada wines with Chef Luis Arce Mota and two other experts in the field at Contenta Nueva York. I still have those notes where we found it, and I described the Blanco 2022 with deep love. I have yet to visit this project in Coahuila. Even so, my dearest cousin, Pedro Rodriguez Cisneros, recently visited Parvada and told me that the project and the location of Vinos Parvada is astonishing, "*esta todo nuevo prima* (it's all new cousin)" like a good *lagunero* (man from La Laguna region), appreciating the evolution of our region.

"The residential complex has lots of 1,000 to 2,000 m2 -approximately 3280.84 square feet, under the shade of a magnificent walnut; in addition, some of its lots have their own vineyard. Parvada has cobbled streets, security and main access booth, underground facilities, fences, and perimeter fences, closed circuit and surveillance system, as well as a clubhouse with swimming pool, two paddle tennis courts, gym, terrace, restaurant-bar, bathrooms, pedestrian walkways, and wide green areas. Complementing its natural design, it has a creek and a large decorative lake". – Vinos Parvada, 2022

In the United States, you can find their Cardenal Blend wines, Caladoc Malbec, Vino Tinto Reserva, White wine, a blend of Verdejo, Chardonnay, and Sauvignon Blanc.

Barro Viejo

Barro Viejo Winery is a family business located northwest of downtown Valle de Parras. Formerly, it was known as *Hacienda La Soledad*, which was founded approximately 150 years ago. It is framed by dry hills but blessed with fertile soil, and its wine production is believed to date back some 200 years ago.

Barro Viejo's story began in 2008 when the vineyard planted Cabernet Sauvignon, Merlot, and Syrah vines. Three years later, the perfect combination of these three varieties resulted in the first bottle of Barro Viejo.

I am interested in tasting their Cabernet Franc and their blend of Merlot and Syrah, which I hope to find in the US soon.

Hacienda

If you already noticed, many of the new wineries have been founded on historic haciendas, *what in the United States we know as fincas that are called differently due to the history surrounding them and the Spanish influence. The* Haciendas *were instituted in the colonial period in México. The workers lived in service houses within the* Hacienda *or areas close to where they were assigned to work.* El Patrón *(the boss), also known as the Landowner, lived on the* Hacienda, *so they were considered different from the workers.*

Hacienda La Florida

Hacienda Florida, a charming vineyard nestled in the northern region of México, takes its name from the historic Hacienda La Florida. The vineyard spans a vast area of 20 hectares and was initially established as a family project in 2012, but since then, it has become a successful multi-investor partnership. That same year, the vineyard planted a range of carefully selected Cabernet Sauvignon, Grenache, Syrah, Malbec, and Mourvèdre vines from France, which have thrived incredibly well in the unique climate and soil of the General Cepeda region of Coahuila.

San Juan de la Vaqueria

Located in Saltillo, the Capital of the State of Coahuila, they are at an altitude of 1,850 meters above sea level with a semi-desert climate, warm and reddish soil, which make San Juan de la Vaquería the ideal place for cultivation and maturation of vines.

They specialize in red wines blends such as Cabernet Sauvignon-Syrah Blend and Cabernet Sauvignon- Syrah to produce wines that have character and express the terroir through winemaking and aging processes in French oak barrels. In this vineyard, you can find white wines based on Verdejo and Moscatel, while their Cabernet and Merlot are blended with reds and house reserve. I have heard they are already available in California, but not in the rest of the United States, but we will be on the lookout.

Mi prima Nayeli Cisneros en Nuevo Parras

Mexican *familias* are big! It is no surprise that I have many *primos y primas* (cousins) from my extended family, both paternal and maternal who I do not even know! I recently find out that I have a cousin that also loves wine. It is funny that we followed each other on Instagram and didn't know we were *primas*! We are second cousins, but still the bond is so strong. His father is my father's first cousin. But also, we connected through wine. Nayeli is younger than me but just as passionate about wine. She is an Architect and also holds a Wine Certificate, WSET 1. She has already visited more than a handful of wineries and has seen the evolution of *Nuevo Parras*, that is, the newest wineries emerging in Coahuila. Therefore, I asked her to share with me some photos from her recent visits to include in this book. She was kind and agreed to share. *¡Gracias Prima!*

Don Leo

I woke up on a weekday in June 2020 to multiple messages from friends and family. I discovered that Don Leo Cabernet Sauvignon was recognized the World's Best Cabernet Sauvignon during the pandemic. I decided to look for the *Concours International Des Cabernets*, which declared it the winner. The wine was a 2013 vintage produced in Valle de Parras, Coahuila, which made me proud. However, I am still waiting to buy it, and I do not know if there are still bottles of this vintage available due to high demand. Don Leo Winery has become famous for creating a great wine experience and for attracting many visitors.

Although I have not been aware of any importers for this winery, their wines are highly sought after in México, so they may not be exporting anytime soon. They also grow Pinot Noir and Syrah.

The winery owes its name to its founder, Don Leo Mendel, originally from Linnich, Germany. He arrived to México and dedicated himself arduously to the agricultural sector, where he developed his love and passion for the countryside. These values were transmitted to his family, who created Viñedos Don Leo in his memory with the same dedication and spirit.

El Asado vs *El Guisado*

There is a completely different culture in northern México almost unknown in the United States and beyond. In México, it is often called *"La Cultura del Asado vs la Cultura del Guisado* (The culture of asado vs the culture of stew)". This means that in the north, in terms of food, there is a whole culture around grilled meat, compared to the south, where the food culture is mainly focused on stews. That is just one of the differences between the culinary culture, but there are many more in terms not only of culture but also soils and altitude, proximity to the US, and other winemaking conditions.

3.2 Central México

Central México is also known or referred to as *El Bajío*. For the purposes of this book, I refer to Central México as the states of San Luis Potosí, Querétaro and Guanajuato, although some importers already include Aguascalientes, but for this endeavor, I consider this as an emerging region.

San Luis Potosí

22.1565 °
100.9855 °
W

San Luis Potosí

Besides wine, I love movies. Who doesn't? But, why am I telling you this? "The Mexican" from 2001, starring Brad Pitt and Julia Roberts, was filmed in Real de Catorce, one of the most beautiful towns in México located precisely in the state of San Luis Potosí.

San Luis Potosí, is located approximately 6000 feet above sea level, being considered one of the highest regions in México.

Important Fact

San Luis Potosí is the smallest wine region in México.

Location

San Luis Potosí is located in central México, nestled just south of the northern states and north of Querétaro and a bit further down in México City. This location is well-connected for transportation in the center of the interior plateau of the country.

Elevation

Most vineyards are located at 5,500-5,700 feet above sea level (Mexican Wine Council, 2022)

Terruño

In San Luis Potosí, three main types of soils are commonly found: sandy loam, clay loam, and silt loam when establishing vineyards. The combined land area used for these vineyards is about 132-134 hectares.

Grapes

- White grapes: Chardonnay, Gewurztraminer, Sauvignon Blanc.
- Red grapes: Cabernet Sauvignon, Cabernet Franc, Grenache, Merlot, Syrah, Sangiovese, Tempranillo and Pinot Noir.

Wineries

There are about 3 to 5 wineries around Moctezuma, San Luis Potosí. I have read that some retailers refer to this region as "Valle de Moctezuma", but I have not seen anything more official. Cava Quintanilla is the most prominent winery in the area. They are famous for their Laberinto series, named for a meditative labyrinth on their property. I have personally tasted some of their wines in New York, and I can confirm that Laberinto Red Blend Nebbiolo and Oak Aged Gewurztraminer are now available in the US.

Queretaro

20.5888 °
100.3899 °
W

Querétaro

Be ready to fall in love with Mexican Fizz! This section is dedicated to my dear friend, Mexican musician and composer Jorge Peart who passed away in 2022. My first visit to Valle de Bernal in Querétaro was with Jorge. We shared more than our year and place of birth, we created extraordinary memories in Central México and México City that forged me to find my place in the world. We both loved music, wine and even when we were both from the north we felt a strong connection to Central México. I only cherished the moments we spent together as a true and most precious friendship.

Tequisquiapan, a *Pueblo Mágico* in the south of Querétaro, has 28 vineyards in Valle de Bernal Wine Route. The cultivation of grape vines is a rarity in this region due to its latitude of about 20 degrees north. Despite conventional theories of viticulture, Querétaro is the southernmost central wine region in the northern hemisphere, 10 degrees further south than that supposed southern boundary of wine production. However, wineries have been thriving for some time and are already looking to produce quality wines in small quantities, mostly.

As I wrote about Querétaro, I found myself overwhelmed with emotion. It really is a magical place. Beyond the Traditional Festival of *Feria del queso y el vino* and its charming, colonial towns, one cannot help but fall in love with the Mexican Fizz!

My First Visit to Finca Sala Vivé

I visited Viñedos Freixenet for the first time in 2007, and honestly, I cannot wait to go back. Many things have changed since then, but knowing this place very early in my adult life made me recognize them later in my years in Spain. This one is a global wine brand that is currently part of the Henkell/Freixenet portfolio, focusing mainly on Spanish wines. Still, they also have fabulous vineyards and a beautiful wine tasting room in Valle de Bernal, México. At that time, I visited some very dear friends and after we took a hike in La Peña de Bernal. We loved their Rosé, Vivanti and the Brut Petillant.

Important Fact

Did you know that the most important production of sparkling wine in México comes from Querétaro?

Location

Querétaro de Arteaga, also known as Querétaro, is located in central México, less than 3 hours north of México City.

Querétaro is one of the smallest states in México. However, it is also one of the most heterogeneous. Its many attractions make it a fascinating, dynamic, colorful, and diverse state. Querétaro can be visited all year round; its good climate makes the stay pleasant, and its many activities make it unforgettable. Tequisquiapan, for instance, is one of the magical towns, also known as *Pueblo Mágico*, declared by Unesco as a world heritage where *La Feria del Queso y el Vino* has been held since the mid-1970s. Such an event is a beautiful wine festival celebrating the area's heritage around wine and cheese every year in the month of may.

Elevation

Most vineyards sit on an average of 6,200 feet above sea level.

Grapes

- White grapes: Xarello, Macabeo, Chardonnay, Sauvignon Blanc, Garnacha, Gewurztraminer
- Red grapes: Cabernet Sauvignon, Malbec, Marselan, Syrah and Tempranillo

Terruño

According to the scientists Cruz de Aquino, M. et al (2012) there are two wine-regions in the central area of Querétaro: San Juan del Río Valley and Tequisquiapan/Ezequiel Montes. San Juan del Río Valley has a semi-dry climate and deep clayey sand soils. Tequisquiapan and Ezequiel Montes have more arid conditions, sloping terrain, and calcareous soils with a hard subsoil layer.

Wine Regions

The Mexican Wine Council recognizes 3 main wine regions in the State of Querétaro: San Juan del Río, Ezequiel Montes y Tequisquiapan. However, this region is also known as Valle de Bernal.

Wineries

By 2022, there are 28 producers in the region. I am highlighting just two of the producers that are available in the US. But there are many wine boutiques growing in Querétaro.

Vinaltura

In 2016, finally, Vinaltura was consolidated as a family project that seeks to actively participate in the greater diffusion, culture, positioning, and responsible consumption of Mexican wine both in the country and internationally.

Vinaltura currently has 6.5 hectares with 11 planted varieties and a production capacity of 24,000 bottles per year. The approach is to prioritize the best quality in each of its products. Vinaltura is making known the potential of Querétaro to become a benchmark for Mexican wine. Some of their whites are already available in the US, such as Blanco Bajío Blend, a Chenin Blanc and their Gewurztraminer.

Freixenet México

Viñedos Freixenet México produces one of the main Mexican sparkling wines. Its name is Finca Sala Vivé, the same as its tasting room, perhaps because Sala Vivé represents the distinctive style of Freixenet México.

However, this style is not available in the US, but Freixenet México together with La Competencia Imports have created a label called "El Bajío" that includes a Sparkling Brut, Sparkling Brut Rosé and Marselan grape-based Red Wine called "Tinto El Bajío" and is available in the United States. If you ever had the opportunity to visit Finca Sala Vivé in Querétaro, please do it.

VIÑA DOÑA
DOLORES
BY FREIXENET MÉXICO

Photo Credit: From left to right, Nayeli Cisneros, mi prima took the first picture in 2022. All the rest were taken by Aide Berenice Cruz in 2007 during our fist visit to Vinedos Freixenet.

There are other outstanding wineries in Querétaro such as De Cote, La Redonda and San Juanito.

"I saw a sunset in Querétaro that seemed to reflect the color of a rose in Bengal" — Jorge Luis Borges

Guanajuato

21.0190 °
101.2574 °
W

Guanajuato

San Miguel de Allende, or SMA for short, is a captivating city in Guanajuato recognized as a UNESCO World Heritage Site. It is known for its magnificent colonial architecture, delicious cuisine, and thriving arts community.

The iconic *Parroquia de San Miguel Arcángel* is a prominent colonial building seen everywhere in the city, evoking a clash of cultures as the community is vibrant and diverse. For an unforgettable experience, take *la Ruta del Queso y Vino* to Guanajuato City, where you can visit charming boutique wineries and enjoy a glass of wine while basking in the warm glow of sunset on one of SMA's picturesque rooftops.

It should be noted that San Miguel de Allende is the only municipality in the country that produces organic industrial grapes, with 48 tons cultivated. This represents 6.77% of the total grape production in the state. (Mexican Wine Council, 2022)

The local government of this region is putting a lot of effort into establishing a wine route and gaining international recognition. The 31st. *Concours Mondial de Bruxelles*, a highly anticipated and recognized event, is scheduled to take place on May 14, 2024 in the charming city of Guanajuato, México.

Location

Central México

Elevation

6,500 – 6,700 feet above sea level

Terruño

Soil: sand and loam clay

Grapes

- White grapes: Sauvignon Blanc, Moscato, Semillon,
- Red grapes: Cabernet, Cabernet Franc, Caladoc, Grenache, Malbec, Merlot, Nebbiolo, Sangiovese, Syrah, Tempranillo

Remarkable story: Annual production for the entire region is approximately 60,000 boxes.

Wineries

There are about 43 wineries in *Valle de la Independencia* (Independence Valley).

Santísima Trinidad

La Santísima Trinidad Winery has multiple vineyards, including San Lucas Vineyards and San Francisco Vineyards. These share a common concept of combining various amenities in one location. They are mainly real estate developments with agricultural areas, including vineyards and olive and lavender fields. Additionally, there is a boutique hotel, polo field, restaurants, olive, and lavender workshops, and a wine workshop. Another development on the property is Los Senderos Vineyards, which includes real estate, a vineyard, and a restaurant.

You might imagine a full-scale wine experience and full-scale winemaking experience by this description, and let me tell you, it really is, and I have yet to visit it. However, one of my best friends has, and he gave me the full scope firsthand. Marcos Guevara has been my friend since day one of college in México, and has been right in the top ten of my best friends, and will be until life do us part, if it does, because friendships like these are hard to forget. I admire Marcos for his brilliance; he is one of the many qualified Mexicans who left their country in search for better opportunities. He moved to New York before I did, but we are still good friends and I value his opinion. When we finally met again in 2020 after the pandemic lockdown, he surprised me with a bottle of Santísima Trinidad and shared his experience at the luxury winery. He described the beautiful lavender fields, olive trees, and wine tasting, which reminded me of the romantic atmosphere of the French wine regions of Rhône and Provençe.

Viñedos Guanamé

Located in Valley de Jaral de Berrios in San Felipe, Guanajuato, Vinos Guanamé was established in 2011 at Rancho Pájaro Azul. The third and fourth generation of farmers and breeders recognized the potential of the land for growing vines at 5,900 feet above sea level due to their passion for wine. Syrah was the first variety planted in 2011, followed by Malbec, Merlot, Cabernet Sauvignon, and Tempranillo in 2012, 2013, and 2014. (Guanamé. Vinos Guanamé. 2023).

Vinos Guaname confidently launched its first label, Syrah 2014, into Mexican market in 2015, paying homage to the land's rich heritage of more than 40 years. Recently, at a Mexican wine tasting organized in New York by La Competencia Imports and La Contenta Oeste, New York, I had the opportunity to taste their Guanamé Red Blend of Malbec, Syrah, Tempranillo, and Merlot. Lucky for you, this wine is available in the United States. Stay tuned for it!

Tres Raíces

Tres Raíces was founded in 2012 with the planting of the first vines to start the production of wines and the construction of the main building in 2016. Subsequently, in October 2018, they received customers in their tasting room facilities.

Tres Raíces, located in the heart of *Bajío*, Guanajuato, has a restaurant specialized in root cuisine and 60 hectares of extensive vineyards. A captivating reflecting pool adds a sensory experience. Other than that, they offer tours of their vineyards, underground cellar, production area, and tastings. (Tres raices, 2023)

Its portfolio available in the US includes a: Grenache Rosé, Nebbiolo, Sangiovese Blend and other Tempranillo based-wines.

Aguascalientes

One of the smallest states in México, bordered to the west, north, and east by the state of Zacatecas and to the south and southeast by the state of Jalisco (Britannica, 2022).

Once, I visited Aguascalientes in high school for a Volleyball tournament -Yes, I once played sports.

I was amused by the magic of old colonial México that surrounds Aguascalientes. They are passionate about the legacy of Spanish traditions, such as *La Feria De San Marcos,* held annually around St. Mark's Day. The celebration in question is undoubtedly one of the most significant and ancient events in México. Every year, for three weeks, usually mid May, the city of Aguascalientes is flooded with tourists who come to enjoy the cultural and artistic programs and the main attraction: *la fiesta de la charrería* (rodeo) events. Wine is also an integral part of the festivities, reflecting the region's rich cultural heritage.

Important Fact

Aguascalientes is the fourth largest wine producer in México.

Location

Central México.

Elevation

Most vineyards are located between 6,100 and 6,200 feet above sea level (Mexican Wine Council, 2022).

Terruño

Its soils are a combination of sand, clay and rocks. There are about 769 to 810 hectares planted with grapes for wine production.

Grapes

- Red grapes: Cabernet, Cabernet Franc, Carignan, Malbec, Merlot, Nebbiolo, Syrah, Tempranillo.
- White grapes: Grenache Blanc, Macabeo, Sauvignon Blanc, Viognier, Chardonnay, Chenin Blanc.

Wineries

There are 18 wineries registered with the Aguascalientes Wine Council. The most outstanding are Vinícola Santa Elena, Finca Renacimiento, Bodegas Origen, Viña Las Cruces, Viñedo Cuatro Soles, just to name a few.

They have excellent documentation on *Ruta del Vino de Aguascalientes* website regarding visiting hours and events en each winery. I hope to see more well-documented resources like this soon for many other wine routes through México.

Congratulations to the Government of the State of Aguascalientes. For more information visit https://rutadelvinoaguascalientes.com.mx/.

Baja California

With Valle de Guadalupe, one, if not the most important Mexican wine region, Baja California is by far one of the largest viticultural zones in the country, accounting for 90% of the country's wine production. However, Baja's temperate climate, which is a result of its proximity to the Pacific Ocean, makes it more appropriate than the warmer regions of México. Actually, the beautiful beaches of Baja California may be its biggest claim to fame. There are large stretches of sand on both sides of its Peninsula, with the Pacific Ocean to the west and *el Mar de Cortez* to the east. Beaches and wine? Does not sound like a paradise to you?

Baja California

30.8406°
115.2838 °
W

The Baja wine route includes wineries from Valle de Tanamá, Valle de Las Palmas, Valle de Calafia and Valle de Guadalupe. Valle de Guadalupe is only one part of the Baja California wine route, since it covers a stretch of highway of more than 70 kilometers. And within Valle de Guadalupe, the highest concentration of winemakers is in the town El Porvenir. From San Antonio de Las Minas to the immediate vicinity of Tecate, there are more roads and secondary roads that branch off to Valle de Guadalupe and other wine-producing communities.

I cannot stress enough that Valle de Guadalupe is the largest wine region on the Baja wine route and where most wineries, restaurants, hotels, and attractions are located.

Elevation

It has an elevation of 1100 feet above sea level. The Mediterranean microclimate of Valle de Guadalupe region, the type of soil, its elevation, and the rainfall conditions favor the development of the vine and wine-growing activity. (Mexican Wine Council, 2022)

Grapes

- Red grapes: Cabernet Sauvignon, Merlot, Mission, Nebbiolo, Petite Syrah, Grenache, Tempranillo
- White grapes: Chenin Blanc, Sauvignon Blanc, Chardonnay

Terruño

Valle de Guadalupe features various types of soil, including sandy loam, granite, and clay. San Antonio de las Minas, near the ocean, is also part of the region. (Wine Enthusiast, 2022)

Wineries

Valle de Guadalupe wineries are located within the wine route, Municipality of Ensenada, Baja California.

The Must-visit Wineries in Valle de Guadalupe!

The entire Valle de Guadalupe is amazing. It is impressive to see how the vines can give such good flavors coming from a practically arid and desert land, vineyards next to the sea give life to Mexican wines with maritime influence.

Producer of approximately 70% of the wines made in México (Mexican Wine Council, 2022), Valle de Guadalupe is an adventure and a discovery. Although it is becoming "mainstream" it is worth a visit, there are wineries and vineyards that you should add to your list of places to visit.

Bodegas Domecq

Bodegas Domecq has been producing wines in Valle de Guadalupe since 1972. It is considered one of the pioneers in Valle de Guadalupe. They recently celebrated their 50th anniversary. Their Red Blend and White Blend, Chateau Domecq, is imported into the US by Gonzalez Byass USA.

Monte Xanic

Monte Xanic Winery was established in 1987 by Eric, Hans, Manuel, Ricardo, and Tomás, who shared a passion for good quality wine and a common goal of putting México on the world map of enology. The winery is located in Ensenada and features impressive architecture, a lake, and a terrace with stunning views for wine tasting. Monte Xanic is a well-known wine brand in México and the East Coast. I highly recommend their Chenin Blanc, Colombard white blend, and red Gran Ricardo. It's worth noting that their Cabernet Sauvignon recently won a Gold Medal at the *Concours Mondial of Cabernets*.

L.A. Cetto

In 1928, Don Angelo Cetto, an Italian immigrant, began growing L.A. Cetto wines. But making great wine takes years in the making. So, in the 1980s, L.A. Cetto wines launched its first varietal line L.A. Cetto.

L.A. Cetto is one of the oldest wineries in Valle de Guadalupe and is the second largest producer of Nebbiolo in the world after Italy. The Nebbiolo L.A. Cetto has won 21 medals internationally.

L.A. Cetto, produces an award-winning Bordeaux-style red wine called Terra. Also, its Cabernet Sauvignon, Petit Syrah, and Nebbiolo are available in the US. Another of its excellent red wines is Merlot Don Luis. I am not usually a Merlot lover, but

Don Luis vintages have silky tannins that make me want more.

With more than a thousand modest hectares and Italian origin, this vineyard is an empire in Valle de Guadalupe. The territorial extension is huge, and also is the production of wines, which means that we can find this label throughout México at affordable prices very accessible. L.A. Cetto also produces more than 20 types of wine and excellent olive oil.

You can find their wines in the United States.

Adobe Guadalupe

La Competencia Imports reports that Tru Miller and her husband, Donald, bought 24 hectares of vineyards surrounded by olive and pomegranate trees in 1997. They collaborated with renowned agronomist Hugo D'Acosta, who at the time was working as a winemaker for Santo Tomás, to start their visionary project. Currently, Daniel Lonnberg works as a full-time winemaker. Their red blends are somewhat in the style of the Rhône named as archangels: Uriel, Miguel, Kerubiel, Serafiel, Gabriel, and Rafael.

If you visit Baja California, this winery is a must. They offer wine tasting, wine tours, accommodation with breakfast, and a shop. The architecture is a mixture of Roman and Hispanic. Just walking around the place worth it.

There are many wineries in Baja California, and you can find other great experiences and architecture, such as Las Nubes, El Cielo, and Bruma, with the most innovative architecture. My only wish when I was there, was to be able to stay longer.

There is another producer that does not have a tasting room in Valle de Guadalupe, but you will find their wines in the US, and I want to provide you a background on Casa Jippi.

Casa Jippi

This fantastic project was created by two families, two wineries, and two valleys. It brings together Rancho Llano Colorado, one of the most important and sought-after grape producers in the area; Vinícola Bruma, a young winery that is pushing the limits of Mexican winemaking; and Lulu Martinez Ojeda, one of the México's leading winemakers who is also one of its outstanding ambassadors abroad. The idea is simple: to produce the best possible wine from the best available grapes at an affordable cost for consumers, giving to the region the recognition it deserves. Casa Jippi's motto is: "Good wine with no added flavor, straight from our vineyard to your table".

Many More Mexican Wine Regions

There are many more Mexican wine regions. Please note that I intentionally left out other regions in this book, such as Chihuahua and Zacatecas. I will visit them again one day and taste their wines.

However, let me tell you about the most unexpected emerging wine region: Nuevo Leon. Through a conversation I had with the agronomist Jaime Cavazos, who led the study on Organic Crops in the state, I found that there were vines growing near Monterrey, México, the place where I grew up.

Nuevo León

Nuevo Leon is a region located in the northeast of México, and it is known for its hot and desert climate. It shares a border with south of Texas. *La Sultana del Norte* is well known for its agricultural efforts focused on growing citrus. Delicious and juicy oranges are grown here. La *Region citrícola de México,* as it is known, covers approximately 900,000 feet from Santiago to Linares.

Nuevo León is also known as a beer-producer state. Heineken México's headquarters and production center are located in Monterrey. Formerly known as Cervecería Cuauhtémoc Moctezuma is now a subsidiary of the Dutch brewer Heineken

(Maddicks, 2016) and produces Carta Blanca, Sol, Dos Equis, Indio, Bohemia, and Tecate portfolio of beers.

With the arid conditions, it is unimaginable to even consider wine production. However, *los regiomontanos*, (citizens of Nuevo Leon), always welcome a challenge. The people of México, my people, are warm and welcoming, but the people of *el Norte*, the people I grew up with, are hard-working people. *La cultura del trabajo* surrounds us.

Therefore, it is not surprising that through some of my best friends in Monterey, I met agronomist Jaime Cavazos who led a pilot grape growing program at the Agriculture Division of the Autonomous University of Nuevo León (UANL, by its acronym in Spanish) between 2015 and 2020. The objective of the program was to study the possibility of growing vines and converting Nuevo Leon into a wine region. Such an ambitious project was called *Cultivos Alternativos* (Organic Crops). The effort of the Cavazos division endeavor was to provide an agricultural alternative for the regional farmers that usually grow oranges. **Valle de Linares**

When I first spoke with Jaime Cavazos in 2020, they had already cultivated three and a half hectares of grapevines in Linares, Nuevo Leon. For the past couple of years, they have been growing Chenin Blanc, Chardonnay, Merlot, Malbec, Syrah, and Cabernet Sauvignon.

In addition to the academic efforts of the Educational Institution, other wineries have emerged in the last decade. For instance, many families have ventured into cultivating their vines. *Mi prima*

Nuevo León

25.5922°
99.9962 °
W

Nayeli told me that she visited Viñedos de Garza Moschen and Don Regulo. In the early stages, they have a family-style approach and although they have already produced a few vintages, she mentioned that she thinks their red wines are promising.

Want to Visit Mexican Wine Country?

If you have already fallen in love with Mexican wines, consider planning your next visit to the Mexican wine region. Although there are pre-established wine routes, it is also essential to consider certain factors when traveling to Mexican wine regions.

But, before traveling to the Mexican wine region, treat your palate to the gift of Mexican wines.

Photo credit: Nayeli Cisneros, 2020

Photo credit: Nayeli Cisneros, 2020

10 Mexican Styles of Wines to try

Friendly reminder: México is a melting pot of grapes.

Lately, Mexican winemakers have had experiences making wines in different places of the world, bringing that knowledge and applying it to our Mexican terroir. For example, Camilo Magoni of Bodegas Magoni brought his Italian heritage and is currently blending Vermentino with Chardonnay, a blend that, for instance, only happens in México. So, as that example of a unique grape pairing, I am suggesting ten Mexican wines to get your feet wet in what they are today. But of course we have to taste the history, so I am also suggest some wines that are essential to try if you want to taste part of the evolution of Mexican wine.

Remember to Experience These Mexican Wines With a Whole Open-Heart.

4.1. Los tempranillos

We cannot deny the influence that México has received from Spain since the sixteenth century. The clash of cultures has influenced many cultural aspects and, of course, viticulture. For example, Tempranillo is a grape native from Spain but was brought to México by the Spanish conquerors or early immigrants. So, let's begin our Mexican wine journey by enjoying some of the producers who have preserved that history in Baja region and were some of the first producers in Valle de Guadalupe. For instance, Bodegas Santo Tomas is one of the first Baja California wineries to include Tempranillo in a red blend even today.

Tempranillo a la Mexicana mixed with Cabernet Sauvignon is what I mean when I say: *"A la Mexicana"*. Naturally, this type of mixing can only happen in México. Tempranillo is used, for example, in other parts of the world, such as Rioja, Ribera del Duero in Spain, or Portugal, to name a few. However, it is blended only sometimes with Cabernet Sauvignon. For example, Tempranillo is the main grape for their *tintos* in Rioja. Even so, they have specific **rules for their quality model that only allow the blending with** Garnacha Tinta, Graciano, Mazuelo, and Maturana tinta.

Los Tempranillos

by Matthew Suarez

by Cesar Fernandez Dominguez

Bodegas Santo Tempranillo Cabernet Sauvignon Red Blend

Winery: Bodega Santo Tomás
Region: Valle de Guadalupe, B.C.

El Tempranillo a la Mexicana

Bodegas Santo Tempranillo Cabernet Sauvignon Red Mix

Winery: Bodega Santo Tomás.

Region: Valle de Guadalupe, Baja California.

Many more wineries have sprung up in the valley in the last 50 years. Nowadays, there are many boutique vineyards in Baja. One of the newer producers, which I mentioned in the Baja California winery section, is Casa Jippi and as already stated, its motto says: "Good wine with no added flavor, straight from our vineyard to your table". Thus, a modern approach to Mexican Nebbiolo features a fruity flair in Casa Jippi Nebbiolo 2020, also called Casa Jipi Red.

4.2. Los Nebbiolos

Nebbiolo wines "are translucent, just like Pinot Noir. They usually have a delicate smell, but when you taste them, you are greeted with robust tannin and high acidity" (Wine Folly, 2022). Nebbiolo is the grape behind big, bold Italian red wines like Barolo and Barbaresco. However, Mexican Nebbiolo might have a different flavor profile.

According to renowned wine writer Karen McNeil, Mexican Nebbiolo can only be similar to Italian Nebbiolo. McNeil states in her iconic wine book, "The Wine Bible" (2015) that 'Leading oenologists here believe that Mexican Nebbiolo is probably not a single variety, but several varieties that were brought from Italy after the Second World War by the Italian winemaker Esteban Ferro. Then at Santo Tomás winery, Ferro's cuttings were apparently stalled at Veracruz port, for a long period, and the identification tags got wet, disintegrated and eventually lost. But the cuttings were planted and collectively were called Nebbiolo'.

Dr. Matthew Horkey and Charine Tan, the wine writers behind ExoticWineTravel.com, confirmed this theory in 2016 with winemakers from Baja California Region. They were on a quest for the Mexican Nebbiolo, according to their article originally shared in Jancis Robinson's website 'Purple Pages' now publicly available on their website. They also point out that the Mexican Nebbiolo makes a darker, less tannic wine than its Italian counterpart. With this research background, it is fair to say that *el Nebbiolo Mexicano* is different from the Italian Nebbiolo. Currently, the Mexican Nebbiolo is grown mainly in Baja California and Aguascalientes.

Hence, let's savor the history of Mexican wine in a glass from the hand of Nebbiolo. By experiencing Mexican Nebbiolo from early producers and comparing it to the profile of the newest producers exhibiting different shapes, we are off on the right foot in the tasting of Mexican wines. So first, let's taste L.A. Cetto Nebbiolo. L.A. Cetto is one of the first producers of Mexican Nebbiolo in Valle de Santo Tomás in Baja. The first time I taste a L.A. Cetto Private Reserve Nebbiolo 2015 was in *Pueblo Mágico* of Santiago, Nuevo León, with my family, and then I paid little attention to the tasting profile. However, I am glad to have tasted it again when I got a sample of L.A. Cetto Private Reserve Nebbiolo 2015 from International Spirits & wines Imports.

Los Nebbiolos

L.A. Cetto Nebbiolo Private Reserve

- Winery: Bodegas L.A. Cetto
- Region: Valle de Guadalupe, B.C.

Casa Jipi Nebbiolo

- Grape: 100% Nebbiolo
- Appellation: Guadalupe Valley, BC
- Region: San Vicente Valley, Baja California Mexico

Los *Nebbiolos*

L.A. Cetto Nebbiolo Private Reserve 2015

Winery: Bodegas L.A. Cetto.

Region: Valle de Guadalupe, Baja California.

In the US, L.A. Cetto is among the most widely available Mexican wines through different importers and distributors. Some of these importers are La Mission and International Spirits & wines.

Nebbiolo Reserva Privada. I have had this Nebbiolo in New York and México many times, it is widely available and recent vintages are ready to drink or keep. The 2018 vintage has an intense red color and a fruity, dry and at the same time velvety flavor.

Casa Jipi Nebbiolo

Grape: 100% Nebbiolo

Appellation: Valle de Guadalupe, Baja California.

Region: Valle de San Vicente, Baja California.

This wine is imported to the US through La Competencia Imports.

My suggested pairing for the Mexican Nebbiolo will be Mexican fajitas or *Carne Asada,* aged cheeses, lamb, or *cabrito.*

Sommelier Alejandra from Vin Butik in México City told me once in 2018 "Nebbiolo from Baja California. Everybody has to taste it"

4.3. Cabernet Sauvignon Mexicano

It was a morning in June 2020 when I received a text from one of my high school friends who knew about my passion for Mexican wines and informed me that Don Leo won best Cabernet Sauvignon in a contest somewhere -Don Leo is located in Coahuila, in northern México.

I was new to Don Leo or *Concours International des Cabernets.* Still, the success of this Mexican Cabernet began to receive a lot of attention and media coverage. It was a significant achievement since, according to Newsweek.com, Don Leo wine outperformed wines from 24 other countries to take the top spot previously held by wines from Switzerland, France, Australia, and Portugal.

Since then, I have been researching some Cabernet Sauvignon from México because there is little information available about this variety in México. However, according to SAGARPA -the organization that envisions agricultural development in México (equivalent or equal to the USDA in the US)- Cabernet Sauvignon is growing in many of México's wine-growing regions like Baja, Zacatecas, Aguascalientes, Querétaro, and Coahuila. So, during our journey exploring Mexican wines, it is worth spending some time to the single-varietal Cabernet Sauvignon.

Cabernet Sauvignon Mexicano

Don Leo Linde Cabernet Sauvignon

Winery: Don Leo.

Region: Valle de Parras, Coahuila.

Follow them on Instagram @vinosdonleo

As an alternative, I also recommend you to taste another historical Mexican producer of Cabernet Sauvignon with a touch of Nebbiolo in their Red blend.

Remember: Bodegas Domecq is one of the pioneers in Valle de Guadalupe; they have worked in that Valle for 50 years.

Photo credit: Nayeli Cisneros, 2020

Photo credit: Nayeli Cisneros, 2020

Photo credit: Nayeli Cisneros, 2020

Chateau Domecq Red Blend

Winery: Bodegas Domecq.

Region: Valle de Guadalupe, Baja California.

This wine is imported into the US through Gonzalez Byass USA.

Casa Madero is also producing an exceptional Cabernet Sauvignon from Coahuila and Monte Xanic recently was awarded with a gold medal from the *Concours International des Cabernets* for its Cabernet Sauvignon that I also recommend you to taste.

Cabernet Sauvignon Mexicano

Don Leo Linde Cabernet Sauvignon

Winery: Don Leo
Region: Valle de Parras, Coahuila

Chateau Domecq Red Blend

Winery: Bodegas Domecq
Region: Valle de Guadalupe, B.C.

4.4. Chenin Blanc Mexicano

According to Nils Bernstein of Wine Enthusiast, Chenin Blanc is the most widely cultivated white wine grape in Baja California, however is also growing and thriving in Tequisquiapan, Querétaro, due to the similarity of the Mediterranean microclimate.

Chenin Blanc is a grape that comes from the Loire Valley, France. Mcneil (2015) wrote that it "arose as a natural cross of Savagnin and an unknown parent". It is an ancestral grape with a very acid profile similar to Sauvignon Blanc.

I am fond of Chenin Blanc style from the Loire Valley, so when I sampled the Mexican Chenin, I could not help but compare them. My first experience with a Mexican Chenin Blanc was with Monte Xanic Chenin Blanc Colombard. I have tasted three vintages from this producer and enjoyed them with my family in México, as well as bringing a few bottles back to New York to pair with Mediterranean cuisine.

Monte Xanic Chenin Colombard

Winery: Monte Xanic.

Region: Valle de Guadalupe, Baja California.

I am still curious how Chenin Blanc got to Valle de Guadalupe. Still, Henri Lurton, owner of Grand Cru Classé, Chateau Brane-Cantenac in Margaux, could be a centerpiece in this exchange. Being Chenin Blanc a French grape, and bringing up the connection between France and México, I am glad I stumbled across Chenin Blanc from Lurton. According to La

Competencia Imports, the Lurton Family is convinced that México has its winemaking potential, the warmth of its people, and the generosity of its land, and they are determined to create one of the premiere wineries in Baja California.

Henri Lurton Chenin Blanc

Winery: Bodegas Henri Lurton.

Region: Valle de Guadalupe, Baja California.

But *Chenin Blanc Mexicano* keeps giving us surprises. Chenin Blanc also grows in the State of Querétaro in Central México. At a recent tasting with La Competencia Imports and Vos Selections portfolio in New York, I tried Vinaltura Chenin Blanc 2020, which has more moderate acidity than its Baja counterparts, but is still to linger in the mouth.

Vinaltura Chenin Blanc

Winery: Vinaltura.

Region: Valle de Colon, Querétaro.

Chenin Blanc Mexicano

Monte Xanic Chenin Colombard

Winery: Monte Xanic
Region: Valle de Guadalupe, B.C.

Henri Lurton Chenin Blanc

Winery: Bodegas Henri Lurton
Region: Valle de Guadalupe, B.C.

Vinaltura Chenin Blanc

Winery: Vinaltura
Region: Colón Valley, Querétaro

4.5. Los Red Blends ó *Tintos Mexicanos*

Since there are no strict rules on the appellation of origin for Mexican wine, and it is only labeled as "Product of México", there is a lot of experimentation in the more prominent wine regions regarding the red blends or *Tintos Mexicanos* as I call them.

Some producers, like Monte Xanic, follow international trends and produce a Bordeaux coupage but with Mexican Terroir. Due to Baja California's proximity to California, where Bordeaux blends are standard, it was natural to try this style. On the other hand, Casa Madero, the oldest winery in Latin America, has produced a classic Red Blend with three of its grapes, which is a must for every wine lover at this point in the history of Mexican Wine. Lastly, Lulu Martinez Ojeda from Bruma Vinícola is adding a velvety Syrah to the red mix and proposing a complex red that is becoming one of my favorites. Many more *Tintos* are being blended in México.

Monte Xanic Gran Ricardo

Winery: Monte Xanic.

Region: Valle de Guadalupe, Baja California.

Red Blend Casa Madero 3V

Winery: Casa Madero.

Region: Valle de Parras, Coahuila.

Bruma Vinícola Ocho Reserva

Winery: Bruma Vinicola.

Region: Valle de Guadalupe, Baja California.

Los Red Blends ó Tintos Mexicanos

Monte Xanic Gran Ricardo

- Winery: Monte Xanic
- Region: Valle de Guadalupe, B.C.

Red Blend Casa Madero 3V

- Winery: Casa Madero
- Region: Valle de Parras, Coahuila

Bruma Vinícola Ocho Reserva

- Winery: Bruma Vinicola
- Region: Valle de Guadalupe, B.C.

4.6. Los Blancos

The Mexican white blends are one of the most emblematic styles of Mexican wine because there is no style. They are very diverse, and depending on the region you pick them up from, different grapes join the blend. One way or another, I believe that Mexican white blends or *los Blancos* are becoming a distinctive way to communicate the essence of the winemaker and the terroir.

For instance, Casa Magoni Chardonnay Vermentino, a blend mixed in equal parts by Chardonnay and Vermentino, is this latter one of the Italian grapes used to produce Whites in Eastern Italy. It is a great way for Camilo Magoni, founder of Camilo Magoni, to express his Italian heritage that permeates his Italian Mexican Winery. On the other hand, take the case of Lucia García Alonso, born and raised in Spain and founder of Parvada, located in Coahuila, which produces a white blend with a typical Spanish grape, Verdejo. This creation also speaks about the winemaker heritage.

Casa Magoni Chardonnay Vermentino

Winery: Bodegas Camilo Magoni.

Region: Valle de Guadalupe, Baja California.

Parvada Blanco

Winery: Parvada.

Region: Valle de Parras, Coahuila.

Casa Jippi Valle San Vincente México Sauvignon Blanc

Winery: Casa Jippi

Region: Valle de San Vicente, Baja California

Los Blancos

Casa Magoni
Chardonnay Vermentino

- Winery: Bodegas Camilo Magoni
- Region: Valle de Guadalupe, B.C.

Parvada Blanco

- Winery: Parvada
- Region: Valle de Parras, Coahuila

Casa Jipi
Sauvignon Blanc

- Winery: Casa Jipi
- Region: San Vicente Valley,
Baja California Mexico

4.7. Los Vinos Espumosos

I have mentioned before that Spain has significantly impacted México, including wine production. It's not surprising that Freixenet, a well-known sparkling wine producer in Spain and around the world, decided to expand its operations to Central México in 1979.

Freixenet established its domicile in México in the state of Querétaro. From the very beginning, they were visionaries recognizing the terroir and climatic conditions for the grapes to thrive. In 1984 they opened their historic Finca Sala Vivé tasting room in Valle de Bernal. Since then, they have received lots of visitors who stop by to have the most beautiful time in one of the *Pueblos Mágicos* of México, La Peña de Bernal.

I was one of those tourists who were passing through. I already told you why Finca Sala Vivé is unique for me. Now I will share with you the importance of the wine produced there. It has the same name as their tasting room, but that could not be another way because Finca Sala Vivé is the main of Mexican sparkling wines.

Finca Sala Vivé Brut stands out for its superior production, dazzling and delicate bubbles, silky palate, and exquisite maturity. Unfortunately for you, this sparkling wine is not available in the United States. However, not all hope is lost because thanks to one of the bravest importers, La Competencia Imports, El Bajio Sparkling, a Mexican bubbly, is made in collaboration with Freixenet México and exported to US. El Bajio Sparkling wine is similar in style to Finca Sala Vivé.

I remember once I bought a Balero wine sparkling in an exquisite black bottle with gold motifs on the label, also made in Valle de Bernal in collaboration with Freixenet. I noticed in the mouth that it was very similar to Finca Sala Vivé. When I read the back label, I discovered that it was produced by Freixenet México.

Hence, my recommendation for you about Mexican sparkling wines is that you taste a Sparkling Wine made by Freixenet México. Whether you visit México and find yourself a bottle of Balero Sparkling wines or have the absolute pleasure of tasting Finca Sala Vivé Sparkling Wine, or buy yourself a bottle of El Bajio Sparkling Brut, enjoy some Mexican bubbles and try to identify the character.

Sparkling El Bajio Sparkling Brut - Valle de Bernal

Winery: Viñedos Freixenet.

Region: Valle de Bernal, Querétaro.

P.S. If you are ever in San Miguel de Allende or on your way to Valle de Bernal, 60 minutes away from San Miguel de Allende, you must visit this iconic tasting room and taste their iconic Finca Sala Vivé Sparkling wine.

Los Sparkling Wines

by Joseph Sorrentino

by olandsfokus

El Bajio Sparkling Brut
Valle de Bernal

- Winery: Vinedos Freixenet
- Region: Valle de Bernal, Querétaro

4.8. Mexican hybrid grapes

Scientists crossed native North American grapes with European species in a laboratory to develop hybrid grapes with desired qualities. These grapes are becoming popular with growers due to their cold hardiness, resistance to pests, diseases, and fungi, and also a general reliability in changing environmental factors. The Smithsonian Museum reports that scientists, growers, and winemakers are experimenting with grape varieties to adapt them to the impacts of climate change.

The wine industry is facing several impacts of climate change affecting grapes. Due to the increase in temperatures, the grapes ripen faster and are more vulnerable to pests and diseases. Forest fires are causing smoke pollution and drought stresses vines.

In some parts of México, there are drought problems, so it is important to consider hybrid grapes since they are more resistant. In México, right now, there are a couple of hybrid grapes growing and thriving. I am putting the spot only on two hybrid grapes. The first one is Marselan, a cross between Grenache and Cabernet Sauvignon. The second one is Caladoc, which is a cross between Malbec and Grenache. Both grapes originated in Languedoc and growing and thriving in Coahuila and Querétaro.

El Bajio Marselan - Valle de Bernal
Winery: La Competencia Imports.
Region: Valle de Bernal, Querétaro.
Parvada Cardenal Joven Caladoc
Winery: Parvada.
Region: Valle de Parras, Coahuila.

The Mexican Hybrid Grapes

El Bajio Marselan - Valle de Bernal

- Winery: Freixenet México / La Competencia Imports
- Region: Valle de Bernal, Querétaro

Parvada Cardenal Joven Caladoc

- Winery: Parvada
- Region: Valle de Parras, Coahuila

4.9. *Los Vinos Rosados Mexicanos*

Mexican Rosé is nothing like your Summer Rosé. I am referring to a Summer from Provence, France; style as we know them in the US, showing a fruitiness taste full of red fruit flavors, very light, crisp, refreshing, and very easy to drink. Mexican Rosé can be smooth and refreshing, but it also offer a bit more texture and layering depending on the grapes and winemaking.

There are many styles of Rosé in México. I have fallen in love with three types ranging from Full to Light Body and I like to recommend five of them so you can have an idea of what Mexican Rosé is, with character but still easy to drink.

Casa Madero V

Winery: Casa Madero.

Region: Valle de Parras, Coahuila.

Grapes: Made from Cabernet Sauvignon.

Tres Raíces Rosé

Winery: Bodegas Tres Raíces.

Region: Guanajuato.

Palafox Natural Rosé

Winery: Bodegas Aldo Palafox.

Region: Valle de Guadalupe, Baja California.

Grapes: 100% Mission (We haven't even talked about the Mission grape in this book, but it was one of the first grapes brought by missionaries that still lives on in México and other Latin American countries).

Los Vinos Rosa Mexicano

Casa Madero V

- Winery: Casa Madero
- Region: Valle de Parras, Coahuila
- Grapes: Made from Cabernet Sauvignon

Tres Raices Rosé

- Winery: Bodegas Tres Raices
- Region: Guanajuato

Palafox Natural Rosé

- Winery: Bodegas Aldo Palafox
- Region: Valle de Guadalupe, B.C.
- Grapes: 100% Mission

4.10. *Los Vinos Naranjas*

Orange Wine is produced in a similar way to red wine, but the production of white wine must remain in contact with its skin, pulp, and seeds. In other words, fermentation with maceration achieves the extraction of tannins, color, texture, and more aromatic precursors.

Orange wines from México cannot be missing from this list. While orange wine is a new global trend, it is not a new style of winemaking. On the contrary, it has been produced for centuries.

However, Orange wine has been on the rise worldwide and is positioned as a new option in the market. There is a lot of curiosity surrounding this style of wine, and some Mexican winemakers have embraced it as well.

I recommend taste skin contact also known as Orange wines from Valle de Guadalupe and Coahuila. The latter is featured mainly by the Spanish origin grape Palomino. This grape arrived to México with *La Conquista* and, of course, from the international Chardonnay variety.

RGMX Orange Wine

Skin Contact Palomino

Winery: RGMX.

Region: Valle de Parras, Coahuila.

Bruma Plan B Chardonnay

Skin Contact Chardonnay

Winery: Bodegas L.A. Cetto.

Region: Valle de Guadalupe, Baja California

Henri Lurton Naranja 2020

Skin Contact Chardonnay

Winery: Henri Lurton.

Region: Valle de Guadalupe, Baja California

Bichi La Gorda Yori

Skin Contact Chardonnay

Winery: Bichi Wines.

Region: Tecate, Baja California

Los Vinos Naranjas

RGMX Orange Wine

- Skin Contact Palomino
- Winery: RGMX
- Region: Valle de Parras, Coahuila

Bruma Plan B Chardonnay

- Skin Contact Chardonnay
- Winery: Bodega Bruma Vinicola
- Region: Valle de Guadalupe, B.C.

Henri Lurton Naranja

- Skin Contact Chardonnay
- Winery: Henri Lurton
- Region: Valle de Guadalupe, B.C.

Bichi La Gorda Yori

- Skin Contact Chardonnay
- Winery: Bichi Wines
- Region: Tecate, Baja California

The Natural Wine Movement in Mexico

The México City bar scene is truly remarkable, with each establishment prioritizing mixology and a broad appreciation for natural wines. In fact, its influence has even reached other cities such as Brooklyn and London. The pandemic has caused an increase in the number of New Yorkers moving to México City, contributing to its recent rise in popularity as a destination for natural wine. Not only Vox has been researching the trend, but also Vogue, Wine Enthusiast, and The Washington Post; all of these media have written about the hype.

Do you think the rumor about natural Mexican wines is just hype? In fact, the demand for these wines is constantly increasing, making them a new staple. While I live in Brooklyn many years ago, I can confirm that both, those who have returned from México City and a great amount of consumers are looking for these Natural Wines. I have even talked to restaurant managers who include Natural Mexican Wines on their menus and see that the trend is becoming a norm. Cheers to Brooklyn.

VINO MEXICANO

Mexican Wine Industry on the Rise

México is at a turning point to obtain recognition as a wine-producing country. **Wine-Producing Country, dixit.** Mexican wine Industry has a promising outlook as recent, but not new. Not new at all.

6.1 The future

A sustainable and competitive wine production is a dream that can be achieved in the long term. The organic and natural production of wines is like going back to the roots, to that soul, and is one of the many crucial points for the future.

As the United States' closest neighbor, México has a great opportunity in wine business. This is not a geographically new fact, but it is imperative to take it into consideration. The United States of America is the world's largest wine market having an important number of regular wine drinkers. In addition, it secures the position of the second largest importer of wine based on its monetary value. However, there are a few factors that need to be developed to ensure that Mexican wines get more shelf space. For example, wine production and marketing practices are still, to some extent, in the early stages of development.

The prosperity of Mexican wine relies on the support of consumers and the curators of restaurant beverages lists. Distributors play an important role in promoting and educating others about the region's wine.

◄ Photo by: Ryan T. McCall / Graphic Design by: Mayra Rodriguez

It is fair to say that consumers in México are drinking more and more Mexican wines compared to two decades ago. A dynamic community of wine enthusiasts is hosting mayor events to promote Mexican wines, such as "*Festival Toma Vino Mexicano*". The wine industry Organizations such as the Mexican Wine Council, Provino, States and Federal Governments are collaborating to expand opportunities and make Mexican wines known in México and the rest of the world. However, there are divergent opinions on this matter.

I remember that in the Summer of 2021, people from the Mexican Wine Industry in the Baja Wine Region, such as Provino, members of the Mexican Wine Council at that time, representatives of La Competencia Imports, Erlinda and myself as part of Latinas Wine Club joined in conversations since we proposed to include the National Mexican Wine Day in the NationalCalendar.com a privately owned media firm in the US.

Although it has not happened yet, I am delighted because the Mexican Federal Government has undertaken a similar effort. In the January 10, 2023 edition of the *Diario Federal de la Federación (*Official Journal of the Federation) the celebration of *Dia del Vino Mexicano* (National Mexican Wine Day) was officially declared as October 7. This Holiday will begin to be celebrated in México in 2023.

As an advocate of Mexican wines of México in the World, I applaud the effort of the Mexican Federal Government to support the Mexican wine industry as a whole.

However, Mexican wine is a controversial topic to discuss in México. First, some might say that the local and Federal Government need to support the fast-growing tourist attractions created around wineries in the Baja California Region. Renowned actor and writer, Carlos Puig expressed his opinion about the latest trends in "Mexican wine and real estate development in Valle de Guadalupe" in 2021. In his analysis, he highlighted a worrying situation that authorities should address: the rapid growth of tourism in Valle de Guadalupe. Puig pointed out that hoteliers, landowners, and real estate developers have been encroaching on agricultural land that should continue to produce wine, which has plagued Valle de Guadalupe for years.

Mexican wine prices is another topic that generates a lot of discussion and controversy within México. Please, keep in mind that many of the tools needed for winemaking are not made in México and must be imported, leading to high production costs. On the top of that, there is a perception: in episodes forty-eight and fifty of *'Descorchando'* podcast, Mexican wine expert, Carlos Solares, mentions that some consumers in México consider the purchase price of Mexican wine as high. Additionally, there are concerns that profits from the industry will be distributed more fairly among those who work the land. Solares explains that several factors contribute to the relationship between price and quality, including the fact that many of the raw materials and machinery used are imported, which increases the cost for consumers.

Mexican Wine importers often face challenges related to price and logistics when importing wine from Central México. Due to the need for an established wine route, they must maintain sufficient sales volumes to ensure consistent inventory levels in the US.

Wow! That was only part of the analysis of the Mexican wine industry today, but it is **only** a summary. Let's continue to explore the opportunities and overall awareness of Mexican wines.

6.2 Opportunities

Factors such as distribution, sales, education or awareness, and travel experiences are some of the opportunities that Mexican wines have to continue supporting the entry into the Global Market.

Factor 1: Improve Distribution Routes

As I previously mentioned, Mexican wine in the United States still has a long way to go in terms of distribution. Even Mexican wine in México has a long way to go, especially in touristic areas where is difficult to find Mexican wines or a variety of them. In general, the most recognized Mexican wine brands with a long tradition are more widely available. Still, many small Mexican boutique wineries need better distribution channels within México, and even more so, in the United States.

Despite this, some committed importers continue to lead the way and spread of *los vinos con Alma*. At the same time, distributors have allowed them to enter to specific markets. However, there is still a lot of work to be done in sales. Even so, there is an opportunity to create synergy between importers, distributors, and restaurants, in general, with the whole hotel industry and recognize the value of Mexican wines. Remember that Mexican wines are sold in a higher price range than those from other countries. It is essential to increase the visibility and popularity of Mexican wine brands in the United States, the largest consumer of wine worldwide.

Factor 2: Distributor Sales Force

I know how challenging it can be to sell Mexican wines as someone who previously wanted to join the wine sales force in New York. However, building a strong sales force will remain crucial since it relies on valuing the past, satisfy the people's search for little-known wine regions and benefit from the connection with the southern neighbor.

Factor 3: Explaining the Mexican Quality System

The current classification and labeling system can evolve since "Vinos de México" seal of Federal Secretary of Agriculture, SAGARPA, is the only one inserted in the wine bottles. Some of the regions have agreed to use a state Level classification as part of their labels, like 'Vinos de Coahuila', but this will evolve as the Local Wine Councils mature and in conjunction with the Mexican Wine Council, the quality and classification system will evolve. Nowadays, Wine in México means fewer restrictions and more variety.

Although Mexican wine is indeed a land of experimentation, it is also an industry that has been working on its expansion in the interior and has been welcomed. This trend is driven by the growing consumer market in the United States, which is composed of alcohol consumers of legal drinking age, including Latino consumers, who are part of the fastest growing demographic group in this country with the highest purchasing power of $3 trillion. Mexican Americans: More than 63% of the US population is of Mexican origin, including Mexican immigrants and Americans who identify as Mexican. In addition, these groups, particularly Millennial and Generation Z consumers, seek an authentic, cultural attachment to a beverage.

For Mexican wines to gain international visibility, it is essential to think about the production areas regulation.

Factor 4: Viticulture Education and Knowledge of Mexican Wines

Another undeniable opportunity is the need for enological education around Mexican wines. It is essential to position and expand the market for Mexican wine brands in the United States as the largest consumer of wine in the world.

It is essential also to focus solely on introducing Mexican wine to new consumers while educating them on the history and quality of the region.

Wines of México should continue to work to increase demand for Mexican wine in the United States by organizing events with distributors, restaurants, bars, and festivals. This initiative also aims to promote cross-border business for all Mexican exports and the hospitality and tourism sectors. Wines of México is actively creating and promoting social media content that encourages consumers to explore all of México's wine producing regions.

With this book, my goal is to spread the history and quality of the region. However, wine trade seminars and media to support consumer outreach are critical. There is a demand for knowledge. As the Founder of Latinas Wine Club, focusing on creating and connecting with the community through the many wine events we have hosted since 2020, I have seen a growing community of Mexican wine enthusiasts who want to learn more about history and quality and see Mexican wines in events with restaurants, bars, festivals, etc.

In this regard, US Hispanic Heritage Month, celebrated annually between September 15 and October 15, presents an excellent opportunity for retailers and restaurants to support Mexican wines. Such a period in time is a unique opportunity where people want to reconnect with their roots. We can explore Baja and other Mexican wines from different regions during this time. Wines from central México are available to some extent in the US, but restaurants and retailers must compile wines from this region for customers to learn about.

Factor 5: Strengthening of Travel Experiences

In addition, there is a huge opportunity to create branded travel experiences for the Mexican wine regions. Many companies and organizations have created wine routes to Valle de Guadalupe or the Baja Wine Region, but there is still a need for Guanajuato, Coahuila, and other regions. Cross border collaboration between companies and individuals can still significantly impact the expansion of Mexican wine tourism.

Wine tourism (enotourism) is an essential part of the cultural aspect that surrounds wine. As a wine lover and traveler, moreover, as part of the fundamental analysis in which I have embarked, the Mexican wine routes of México are crucial to make our wines visible to the eyes of the world.

Unfortunately, there is little information about wine tourism in México. In this regard, the Mexican academics De Jesus Contreras and Thomé-Ortíz (2019) analyze the state of knowledge of wine tourism in México through a review of the main academic contributions and the most outstanding cases of wine routes in other parts of the world. In their conclusions, they highlight private companies and local governments that have tried to promote the development of wine regions through the implementation of wine routes.

The projection of wine regions internationally has had, as prominent component, the opening of wineries to tourist activity.

To date, there are Wine Routes in Baja California, Aguascalientes, Querétaro and Coahuila. The emerging wine routes in Guanajuato and San Luis Potosí, and Zacatecas will continue to boom. Proper road signage, guided tours and information should continue to grow in the coming years.

Factor 6: Expansion of Mexican Wines in the Global Market

Are Mexican wines ready to meet the demand of the global market?

Most of the wines produced in México continue to meet domestic demand, which means less wine is available to be exported. However, importers to the US, such as Primo Imports, La Competencia Imports, and La Mision Associates, are working hard to trace the import route to the US. I am also aware of other Mexicans abroad, particularly in London, trying to achieve the same result.

Mexican wine exports are significantly low compared to other countries. For example, México's wine industry must catch up with that of Italy, the world's leading wine exporter. In 2018, Italy exported 19.6 million hectares, while México only exported 10,000. (Mexican Wine Council, 2022)

Mexican wine export routes are complex, non-existent, historically driven, and still face challenges in terms of production available for export. The Mexican wine industry has yet to reach a high point, but it is certainly on the right track as more opportunities emerge.

¡Eso es todo, amigos!

Over time, México has evolved from being just a wine producer to satisfy national demand to an Industry that will consolidate in the coming years. First, México, as a wine producer, will continue to be a melting pot, constantly innovating. Secondly, the Mexican wine industry will consolidate and continue to strengthen the different actors that make it up.

For example, I have heard that Merlot and Malbec varieties also thrive in central México, but I still have many more wines to taste. Also, I was encouraged to taste Moscatel from Guanajuato and Sauvignon Blanc. Those types of wines have my full attention now, and look forward to taste them sooner rather than later. So, if you come across this or any other Mexican wine, give it a try even if it is not on this list. Share Mexican wines with your family and friends.

You might think that our choices produce a small impact, but any decision goes a long way. Please help me spread the knowledge and history of these excellent quality wines with soul and a beautiful tradition that continues to expand.

This identity that I try to communicate, is part of the Mexicans themselves, and must be shared throughout the Americas. I invite you to pair each dish with different Mexican wines, not just Mexican food. How about a Mexican Tempranillo with a hamburger, or why not a delicious pizza with an excellent Mexican sparkling wine? Dare to try all kind of dishes with delicious Mexican wines.

There are many more challenges and opportunities for the Mexican wine industry. This book has been self-funded, and with limited time, I hope to revisit it and give you a brighter perspective on the distribution of Mexican wines around the World. I am confident that Mexican wines are in the eyes of the world, and will soon fill many American glasses.

I hope you have fallen in love with the Wines of México!

What are my next steps?

Advocating for the Mexican wine regions globally is essential, particularly in English. While the Spanish-speaking community in the US and Europe prefers to consume information in their native language, it is crucial to share it in English to reach a broader audience.

A few years ago, I used to travel more frequently between México and New York bringing back a lot of bottles of Mexican wine that were not available in the US market. I am very active on social media, and my followers expressed an interest in learning more about the region. Since the audience was interested in Mexican wines, I started another social media profile, instagram.com/winesofmx and Facebook.com/winesofmx, where I share more about Mexican wines in the US. The growing audience interested in learning about this, tends to interact frequently and consistently with my content.

Social media is a great tool to connect with others who are enjoying in person wine experiences, like wine tastings and dining at Mexican wine restaurants. It is a resource we did not have before and one that many other wine regions around the world use to connect with younger generations who prefer social media to traditional media. By engaging with their communities and seeking recommendations or reviews, these wine regions can remain relevant and accessible to new audiences.

However, social networks are a medium, but Google is still the king of content. Actually, in 2023, Google has 321,000,000 results regarding Mexican wine. There is a need to know more about Mexican wines. Other journalists have also been interested in discovering the richness of *Los Vinos con alma*.

I have launched a website to keep up with the growing demand for information on Mexican wines: *Los Vinos con Alma*. This website is privately owned and is not related to the Mexican Wine Council. I am growing as consultor for Mexican Wine Lists, Mexican Wine Tasting Events, and the release of updated information about *los vinos de México.*

Visit us at winesofmexico.org

Acknowledgments

I wrote this book entirely from New York, but many people write the Modern History of Mexican wines on a daily basis in the Mexican fields and throughout all wine production. I hope more profits comes to our *campo Mexicano* and for the tourism industry to bring it to our communities.

Se de dónde vengo y a dónde voy.

Gracias a mi familia. They have always been with me, empowering me, despite the distance, you all live *en mi corazón y mi mente todo el tiempo.*

Gracias Mamá, la disciplina y la benevolencia a través de tu apoyo y amor incondicional han sido un gran fundamento en mi vida. Te quiero mucho.

Gracias Papá, for the love for books you instilled in me since you took me to that first book fair. I just wish Anthony would be inspired by libraries too.

Para ambos, thank you for those thousands of trips between Torreón and Monterrey and then from Monterrey to the other side of Río Grande.

Those experiences on both sides of *El Rio Bravo* shaped my bicultural life and my interest in how our cultures are connected more than disconnected.

Bro, Moy, thank you for your help fact-check!

Hermana ¡si salió! Con muchas horas de esfuerzo, tu eres mi ejemplo ahora ¡si se puede!

Luan, *dashuria ime,* your love allows me to flourish and sustains me daily. Thank you for your patience and kindness. I survived many whole nights writing this book while you care of the little one. *Unë jam në borxh të përjetshëm me ju.*

Para mis tías, thank you for always cheering me up. *Gracias Tia Cathy, Tia Yadira, Tia Ada, Señora Angélica,* your kind words are engraved in my heart *siempre. Gracias Tío Tito eres como mi segundo padre y por recibirme en tu casa de Texas tantas veces, esas experiencias bilingües y biculturales me han servido mucho a lo largo de mi vida.*

Many thanks to the Consulate of México that has always supported my initiatives, especially Karla Bueno and María Fernanda, Consul of Economic Affairs in New York.

I am very grateful to Chef Luis Arce Mota for constantly trusting me, and inviting me to taste so many Mexican wines to experience the construction of the most extensive Mexican Wine list. Chef, I admire your perseverance which is crucial because you sets an example for many other restaurants that do not even have Mexican wine on their list. *Por la Cultura, ¡Vamos Adelante!*

My dear Bere, you have understood my words, ideas, and concepts and have created excellent designs with them for almost 20 years. I owe you the design of this book. Before wine infographics, there was music and travel. I will never forget when we visited Freixenet México with our dearest Jorge Peart; now he is in a better place. *Me atrevo a decir* that our lives changed that day.

La Competencia Imports, Primo Imports, and Gonzalez Byass Familia De Vino, importers of Mexican wines, thank you for doing the hard work on building those wine routes. I admire and respect your business.

At Latinas Wine Club, I want to thank my one and only partner, Cynthia Rodriguez, you have been the most wonderful cheerleader, and your words are full of kindness and good energy. I appreciate you beyond measure. Thanks to ex-partner Erlinda Doherty, the dream we once had with *los vinos con alma* lives on. We might cross paths in the near future!

Many *amigas* like Mely Ko and Mary Cavazos introduce me to another friend Jaime Cavazos, then Nayeli Cisneros, *mis primos* and my best friends Meli, Marcos, Pablo, Paco, Ricky for being a family network in New York.

Last but not least, I have been trying to write this book for a couple of years, Deyanira and Alba from *Mujeres que se Atreven*. *Por el apoyo incondicional* and encouragement when it was most needed. Your help made this book a reality!

Thank you to you, lover of Mexican wine for appreciating these stories of *los vinos con alma.*

By reading this book, you should be confident that Mexican wine is not an emerging wine region, as it has been produced for 200 years. Please taste more than one Mexican wine.

As a blogger and now as a writer, deep in my heart I knew that sharing a few photos of Mexican wines on my Instagram channel was not enough. Now, the social media pages are dedicated to widespread awareness of the wines of México and will continue to feature tasting notes, love, and education about Mexican wine regions.

Continue your Mexican wine journey there. Join our Mexican wine social media channels

Instagram.com/WinesofMx and Facebook.com/winesofmx or the website winesofmx.org

We are facing a Mexican wine revolution!

¡Qué suerte es estar viviéndola!

Glossary

- Enotourism: Tourism focused around wine regions, wine areas
- Enologist: also known as Winemaker
- Hybrid grapes: grape varieties resulting from crossing two or more species.
- Terroir: Soil, in Spanish is known by "*Terruño*" and better known by the French word *Terroir*
- *Vitis Vinifera*: The grape variety that is predominantly used to produce standard or high-quality wines

About the author

Martha Cisneros Paja

Martha Cisneros Paja is the founder and writer behind WineDiva.com, CEO of Latinas Wine Club, Technology Engineer, a certified WSET 2, Certified Sherry Specialist and professional wine studies student.

She graduated with a College Degree in Engineering with a focus on Information Technologies. Her *Alma Mater* is Instituto Tecnológico de Estudios Superiores de Monterrey (ITESM), known as MIT of México, according to the New York Times. She continued her professional studies by completing a Master's Degree in Information Sciences and Knowledge Management. With 15 years of a prosperous career, she is a lifelong learner and now is immersed in the enjoyment of wine and professional studies.

She holds a WSET 2 diploma with merits and is a Certified Sherry Specialist. In addition, she is a student of the Italian Wine Scholar of the the Wine Scholar Guild. In addition, recently the Court Master of Sommeliers awarded her the Scholarship to take the Introduction to Sommelier course. Moreover, she defines herself as a wine lover.

She is a versatile professional and entrepreneur. In 2020, in the midst of the pandemic, she founded Latinas Wine Club Inc., a community and technology platform with wine education as the *Corazon* (Heart) of the initiative where we want to Educate. Empower. Elevate yourself through Wine.

Her unique perspective has attracted an audience of 17,000 followers around the world. In New York, she hosts wine tastings for the community and personal clients. She has been recognized by Media as a unique and culturally aware voice for wine-loving millennials.

Currently, she is focused on tasting different wine regions, studying for the Sommelier exam, and polishing her writing skills by providing wine recommendations on the blog and Instagram.

Follow her wine journey at winedivaa.com

@winedivaa

@winedivaa

@WineDivaa

Selected References

Barro Viejo. Nosotros. Nosotros. Barro Viejo. México https://barroviejo.com.mx/nosotros/

Barrientos, Jorge. Historia moderna de los vinos de México. Vinos de México. Wine Society México. Junio 2018. Monterrey México, Lecture.

Belding Wayne. The Earthly Underpinnings of México's Vineyards. Winereviewonline. August 22, 2017. USA. http://www.winereviewonline.comWayne_Bleding_on_Mexico.cfm

Bernstein Nils. Wine. With Distinctive Terroir and Varied Microclimates, México's Baja California Aims to Preserve its Character. Wine enthusiast companies. 2023. USA. https://www.wineenthusiast.com/culture/wine/baja-california-mexico-wine-guide/

Bodegas del Viento by Qvoz. Vinos. Nuestros vinos. Bodegas del viento. México. https://bodegasdelviento.com/vinos.html

Bodegas del Viento. Nosotros. Bodegas del viento. BV. México Missed data: 1. Author 8. Publication date https://bodegasdelviento.com/nosotros.html

Bodega los cedros. Nosotros. Bodega los cedros. Bodega los cedros. 2023. México.

Britannica, The Editors of Encyclopedia. "Aguascalientes". Encyclopedia Britannica, 19 Jun. 2021, https://www.britannica.com/place/Aguascalientes-state-Mexico. Accessed 29 June 2023.

Calva, Araceli. Conoce más sobre el vino mexicano a través de este libro. El Universal. 2022. México https://www.eluniversal.com.mx/menu/conoce-mas-sobre-el-vino-mexicano-traves-de-este-libro/

Carion Benoit. Concours Mondial de Bruxelles. The 31st Concours Mondial de Bruxelles will be held in Guanajuato México. The United Nations of fine wines. May 14, 2023. USA. https://concoursmondial.com/en/the-31st-concours-mondial-de-bruxelles-will-be-held-in-guanajuato-mexico/

Contreras De Jesús Daniel, H Thomé Ortiz - RIVAR (Santiago), 2019 Turismo enológico y rutas del vino en México. Estado del conocimiento y análisis de casos https://www.scielo.cl/scielo.php?pid=S0719-49942019000200027&script=sci_arttext

Consejo Mexicano Vitivinícola. LA INDUSTRIA VITIVINÍCOLA MEXICANA EN EL SIGLO

XXI: RETOS ECONÓMICOS, AMBIENTALES Y SOCIALES. CIATEJ. Consejo mexicano vitivinícola. 2022. México https://uvayvino.org.mx/wp-content/uploads/2022/08/industria-vitivinicola-version-final-19-julio-2022-con-portada.pdf

Cruz-de Aquino, Mario A. de la, Martínez-Peniche, Ramón A., Becerril-Román, A. Enrique, & Chávaro-Ortiz, Ma. del Socorro. (2012). Caracterización física y química de vinos tintos producidos en Querétaro. Revista Fitotecnia mexicana, 35(spe5), 61-67. Recuperado en 28 de junio de 2023, de http://www.scielo.org.mx/scielo.php?script=sci_arttext&pid=S0187-73802012000500013&lng=es&tlng=es.

Exotic Wine Travel. Mexican wine. Mexican Nebbiolo from Baja California. Exotic wine travel. December 3, 2016. México. https://www.exoticwinetravel.com/mexican-wine-nebbiolo/

Gobierno de Querétaro. Inicio. Descubre Querétaro Información general e historia del Estado. Poder ejecutivo del Estado de Querétaro. 2022. México. https://portal.queretaro.gob.mx/info_queretaro.aspx?q=CoZUwi4N3J0a+x222RrdKQ=

Global Data. "México - Wine". Wine in México, GlobalData Ltd., 2006. Gale Business: Insights, link.gale.com/apps/doc/A156814249/GBIB?u=nysl_li_scls&sid=bookmark-GBIB&xid=33c1f829. Accessed 19 May 2023. USA

Hacienda Florida El viñedo. Historia del viñedo. Hacienda Florida. 2023. México https://haciendaflorida.com.mx/pages/el-vinedo

Hatchet, Caroline. The U.S. Chefs and Restauranteurs Embracing Mexican Wine. Wine Enthusiast. May 2023, USA. https://www.wineenthusiast.com/culture/wine/mexican-wine-restaurants/

Haz Turismo en Coahuila. Index. Coahuila y sus vinos. Haz Turismo de Coahuila. 2019. México. http://hazturismoencoahuila.com/index.php

International Organization of vine and wine. Highlights. OIV. USA. https://www.oiv.int/

Kuta Sarah. Science. Are Hybrid Grapes the Future of Wine? Smithsonian magazine. September 19, 2022. USA. https://www.smithsonianmag.com/science-nature/are-hybrid-grapes-the-future-of-wine-180980642/

La Competencia Imports. Red wines. Casa Jipi Nebbiolo 2020. La Competencia Imports. 2023. USA https://www.lacompetenciaimports.com/product/Casa-Jipi-Nebbiolo2023

México Selection by Vinopress. Concours Mondial de Bruxelles. Home. Coahuila. Vinopress. 2023. México. https://mexicoselection.com/en/coahuila-de-zaragoza-mexicos-winemaking-strength/

México Selection by Vinopress. Concours Mondial de Bruxelles. 2023 México https://mexicoselection.com/en/

Morris Seren. U.S. The Best Cabernet Sauvignon Wine Comes From...Mexico. Newsweek. September 6, 2020. USA. https://www.newsweek.com/don-leo-mexican-wine-best-cabernet-sauvignon-gold-trophy-cidc-competition-1509557

Paz Octavio. Labyrinth of Solitude. Mexican masks. Groove press, Inc.1961, New York. https://wedgeblade.net/files/archives_assets/13759.pdf

Potencial uva. Planeación agrícola nacional. SAGARPA. 2017. México https://www.gob.mx/cms/uploads/attachment/file/257085/Potencial-Uva.pdf

Puig Carlos. Política ¿A alguien le importa el vino mexicano? Milenio. October 8, 2021. México. https://www.milenio.com/opinion/carlos-puig/duda-razonable/a-alguien-le-importa-el-vino-mexicano_

Querétaro Travel. Inicio. Feria del queso y vino 2022. Secretaría de turismo. 2022. México https://queretaro.travel/lugares/feria-del-queso-y-el-vino-2022/Rivero González. Nosotros. Visión. RG. México https://rgmx.mx/pages/nosotros#vision

San Juan de la vaquería. Nosotros. San Juan de la vaquería. México https://sanjuandelavaqueria.com/

Shmal John P. Coahuila. Indigenous Coahuila de Zaragoza: Land of the Coahuiltecans. Indigenous México. September 6, 2019. USA https://indigenousmexico.org/coahuila/indigenous-coahuila-de-zaragoza/

Serendipity wines. 2020 – 2023. USA. https://serendipitywines.com/catalog/filters/d981c18664b974ffc6d4e568733acbaf/

Texas Border facts. Del Rio Tx. Texas Department of transportation. 2018. USA. https://ftp.txdot.gov/pub/txdot/move-texas-freight/resources/fact-sheets/border/del-rio.pdf

Vinos Parvada. Inicio. Un proyecto integral. Parvada. 2023. México. https://parvadacv.mx/

Vinos Parvada. Our Winemaker Lucia Garcia Alonso. Vinos Parvada. México. https://vinosparvada.com/en/pages/our-winemaker

Whitley Robert. Baja California a Land of Sun, Surf, Sand and ...Wine?. Wine Review Online. 2023. USA http://www.winereviewonline.com/printArticle.cfm?articleID=191

Williams Janice. Feature. Mexican Wine is on the Rise. Pix, February 10,2022, New York, NY USA. https://pix.wine/the-drop/mexico-wine-scene/